I0412476

After The Call

After The Call

The Life of the Minister

Richard C. Anderson

Copyright © 2011 by Richard C. Anderson.

ISBN: Softcover   978-1-4628-6033-3
              Ebook   978-1-4628-6034-0

All rights reserved. No part of this book may be reproduced or transmitted in any form or by any means, electronic or mechanical, including photocopying, recording, or by any information storage and retrieval system, without permission in writing from the copyright owner.

All scripture quotations are taken from the King James Version (KJV) of the Holy Bible except where otherwise indicated.

To contact the author for book signings or speaking engagements, please send email to: *comeLJ@aol.com*
Or *richardanderson4@mac.com*

This book was printed in the United States of America.

To order additional copies of this book, contact:
Xlibris Corporation
1-888-795-4274
www.Xlibris.com
Orders@Xlibris.com
98476

CONTENTS

This book is dedicated Rosalynn Anderson because of what she said on 111th Street and to Dr. Thom Roby teacher, mentor and friend. And my father Walter Anderson

PREFACE

Ever since I was a student at the Kennedy-King Jr. College in Chicago my philosophy professor and great mentor Dr. Tom Roby has encouraged and prodded me to write a book. I believe I can immodestly say I am living an interesting life including a varied academic career from a city college, law school and seminary. From my experiences in Vietnam to my experiences as minister—both very interesting and stressful at times. But each time I began to write I could not find a context for my thoughts and experiences.

Then my Lord and savior Jesus Christ came into my life. And now there is a context into which to place these experiences. God has been at work in my life behind the dim unknown keeping watch above His own. His plan has been unfolding and I believe there are issues I can discuss that have a larger context. The focus of this book of essays is Jesus and the issues that center on ministry.

INTRODUCTION

What is it like to be a minister? What are some of the issues a called man or woman faces? What are the political imperatives of a person dedicated to upholding the gospel and the ordinances of our Lord and Savior Jesus Christ? These are some of the issues addressed in the following pages. Is election and predestination unfair? What about sovereignty verses free-will? There is no need to wait on that one I am a sovereignty man all the way! I do not claim to have the answers to these questions but I am very opinionated and I believe my opinions are biblically sound albeit controversial. Some essays deal with issues of general interest to the Christian life. Issues such as what is the obligation of a Christian to forgive another Christian who has unjustly treated him or her or offended him or her? Is the obligation to forgive absolute or conditional? What about homosexuality in society and the church? Is it a sin to be a homosexual? Is Islam a violent religion or not?

I am sure these essays will evoke strong reactions from the reader. But that is not my primary aim. The Christian life is wonderful. It is not always a happy life but it is always a joyful life. It is a life filled with supernatural wonder and love. Christianity is not a set of beliefs but a love affair. It is a love relationship between us and our God. It is knowing for sure that God loves us—and likes us (1 Chron 28:4). It is my primary aim to convey some of the wonder, love and humbling emotion of the relationship between our God and us His children. And to amplify that by examining the life of one called to offer that love to the world. It is an honor and grave responsibility to be called by God to preach and teach his word to the world. I know that there are other ministries besides preaching and teaching but these are the ministries God laid upon me so that is my focus.

Elder Richard C. Anderson

THE CALL GOD'S CHOICE

Television evangelist Creflo Dollar said something interesting on his program a few years ago that I don't think I will ever forget. He said he woke up one morning feeling very good about his ministry and all he had accomplished. Then the Lord spoke to him and said: "You were not my first choice for this ministry. You were number four. Those other men fell by the wayside." This was a humbling experience to say the least.

That caused me to think about our calls to service and ministry. I have met people in my professional life who have told me that when they were young they felt a call to the mission field or some other ministry but they resisted and went into some other profession. They all expressed regret that they did not follow God's call to ministry. How do these people fit into God's plans for who will serve Him as well as His kingdom on earth? Here are some thoughts on this subject.

> *"The Jonah Call is where God intends for you and only you to carry out His commands."*

TWO CALLS

First: The Esther Call

It seems to me that scripture reveals at least two kinds or categories of calls God places on our lives. One is what I call the Esther Call. Remember Mordecai's words to Esther: *"For if thou altogether holdest thy peace at this time, then shall there enlargement and deliverance arise to the Jews from another place; but thou and thy father's house shall be destroyed: and who knoweth whether thou art come to the kingdom for such a time as this?"* (Esth. 4:14)

Mordecai was saying that Esther was called for this work but if she did not take up the cause of her people, God would carry out His plans by other means—probably with another person. God's will is never thwarted

13

(Isa. 46:10). If you resist the call of God on your life He will call someone else to the ministry He first planned for you. Either way God's intentions will stand and be accomplished.

Second: The Jonah Call

There is also another kind of call—I call it The Jonah Call. The bible says: *"[1] Now the word of the LORD came unto Jonah the son of Amittai, saying, [2] Arise, go to Nineveh, that great city, and cry against it; for their wickedness is come up before me. [3] But Jonah rose up to flee unto Tarshish from the presence of the LORD, and went down to Joppa; and he found a ship going to Tarshish: so he paid the fare thereof, and went down into it, to go with them unto Tarshish from the presence of the LORD."* (Jonah 1:1-3)

We all know what happened to Jonah. After his harrowing experience on the ship and being swallowed by the great fish Jonah submitted to God's call and went to Nineveh. There he delivered an eight word sermon ("*Yet forty days, and Nineveh shall be overthrown.*" Jonah 3:4) and God saved the entire city (Jonah 3:10). When Jonah fled to Tarshish God could have called someone else. But for God's own reasons He determined that Jonah would be the one to preach to Nineveh. The Jonah Call is when God intends for you and only you to carry out His commands. The service or ministry is for you alone and you WILL respond; sooner or later. I guess the motto for the The Jonah Call is: 'Make it easy on yourself,' obey now and avoid the big fish. If you are subject to a Jonah Call you will heed the call. As God said when He called Paul: "*It is hard for thee to kick against the pricks.*" (Acts 9:5) In other words Paul: 'don't try to resist this call.'

Failure to heed an Esther Call results in a lifetime with a sense of loss or even regret. Failure to heed a Jonah Call results in who knows what. I shudder to think. But before it's all over you will go to Nineveh. When my will and His will are the same success is assured "for who hath resisted his will?" (Rom 9:19) Nobody has, not even me.

WHY ME—WHITEWELL

There is a great church in Belfast Northern Ireland called the Whitewell Metropolitan Tabernacle (*www.whitewell.com*). It is a mega church with membership in the thousands which is extraordinary for a church in Europe. My wife and I have worshiped there and met and talked with the pastor a great man of God named Dr. James McConnell. Dr. McConnell is an interesting mixture of humility and—authoritarianism. He is a personally humble man but his concern for the people of God he pastors leads him to exercise strict control over every aspect of the church. For example there is no moving around by the congregation during the sermon. No getting up to leave during the message. No talking and no one leaves during the altar call.

> "... it is easier to accept that God loves then that God also likes us. But He does."

On one occasion pastor McConnell related a conversation he had with some young pastors visiting him. He said they ask him "what is the key to the success of your ministry and the great growth of the Tabernacle?" Dr. McConnell replied there was no key. They said there must be some rule of ministry or some principle of church growth you have applied to account for the thousands of members and your influence in Ireland. Dr. McConnell insisted there was no principle. He said it "just happened." They said "but why?" Why did God bless you?" Dr. McConnell said: "because He liked me!" It's just that simple.

They were chagrined at this answer and skeptical. Pastor McConnell gave the scriptural basis for the statement. He cited 1 Chron 28:4 where David says: "*Howbeit the LORD God of Israel chose me before all the house of my father to be king over Israel for ever: for he hath chosen Judah to be the ruler; and of the house of Judah, the house of my father; and among the sons of my father he liked me to make me king over all Israel."*

This is one of those scriptures I have read many times and never noticed its unique wording. God liked David! Yes David was a man after God's own heart. (1 Sam 13:14; Acts13:22) and he "found favour before God." (Acts 7:46a) It is also true that *"David did that which was right in the eyes of the LORD, and turned not aside from any thing that he commanded him all the days of his life, save only in the matter of Uriah the Hittite."* (1 Kings 15:5) But the simple fact is that God liked David. Why has the Apostolic Church of God grown 20,000+ members under the late Bishop Arthur M. Brazier? God liked Bishop Brazier. God's favor was upon these men and others who have been 'successful' in ministry.

Have you ever asked the Lord "Why are you so good to me Lord? Why have you blessed me so much when I know how I have failed you over and over?" I did ask and God spoke to me plain and clear: "Because I love you Richard." I get a lump in my throat just remembering that moment. Have you ever wondered why God called you into the ministry? Have you ever wondered why God recompenses tribulation to them that trouble you? (2 Thess. 1:6; cf. Luke 18:7) In other words why does God punish people who hurt you? Because he likes you and you are precious in his sight. You are His precious jewel (Mal 3:17) and he places great value on you. God delights in you. (Prov. 11:20; 12:22). When you preach God enjoys your sermons. When you witness God delights that you speak well of His Son Jesus. Ironically I think it is easier to accept that God loves, then that God also likes us. But He does.

When we face the holy God we feel so unworthy. As Isaiah said when he saw the Lord high and lifted up: *"Then said I, Woe is me! For I am undone; because I am a man of unclean lips, and I dwell in the midst of a people of unclean lips: for mine eyes have seen the King, the LORD of hosts."* (Isa. 6:5) And this is the appropriate reaction to the presence of God. But I am suggesting that we also appreciate how precious we are to God. He gave His son to die for us. As Peter said: *"But ye are a chosen generation, a royal priesthood, an holy nation, a peculiar people; that ye should show forth the praises of him who hath called you out of darkness into his marvelous light."* (Peter 2:9) And after calling you out of darkness He further called you to be a minister His messenger of the Good News.

We must be humble in God's sight but we can also rejoice that we are precious to God. Yes, we are dust. (Ps 103:15) We are jars of clay. But we are jars of clay that contain a precious treasure the Gospel entrusted to us by our loving Father. (2 Cor. 4:7-8) God loves us, we are precious to Him and he likes us. There are aspects of our personalities that delight Him. Sure, we exasperate Him at times and try His patience. But through it all he never stops liking us. How about that?

IS ISLAM A VIOLENT RELIGION?

It is important that the minister of the Gospel of Jesus Christ be at least conversant with the teachings of other major religions. In the present geopolitical climate this is particularly true of Islam. This essay discusses in a cursory way the question of whether Islam teaches violence against those who do not practice Islam. We have all seen the articles and discussions on talk shows about whether Islam is a religion that teaches or endorses violence against non Muslims. Some experts cite passages in the Qur'an that call for living peacefully with persons of other faiths. Yet others cite passages calling for the destruction of all infidels. Which view is the truth? This short article will not answer that question but I offer one possible explanation for this apparent discrepancy.

The Qur'an like any complex book of doctrine or philosophy is subject to rules of interpretation. These rules must be applied correctly to understand its teachings. This is true of the Bible and the study of Bible interpretation called hermeneutics. One principle of interpretation some Muslim scholars apply to the Qur'an is the principle of *nasikh*, which holds that later passages in the Qur'an supersede or abrogate earlier ones and negate them (See: *The Truth About Islam* by Ted Haggard, Ministries Today magazine, November/December 2002).

> *"Many people use its text to vindicate their preconceived notions, as is done with the Bible."*

Mr. Haggard cites the following example. There are as many as 114 verses in the Qur'an that call for living peacefully with nonbelievers. These verses were written during a time when Muhammad was militarily weak and had few follows. Later passages calling for violence against idol worshipers (unbelievers) were written when he was militarily strong and had a larger following. These verses according to the principle of *nasikh* supersede and override the older peaceful verses.

This principle applies irrespective of where the verses appear in the Qur'an. For example in Sura 9:5 (009.005) which is near the beginning of the Koran (Quran) contains the following language: ". . . *you may kill the idol worshipers when you encounter them,* punish them, and resist every move they make." (Dr. Khalifa's translation of the Quran, *www. submission.org/suras/sura9.htm*) This was one of the last texts written. Thus the Koran (Quran) contains both peaceful and warlike verses and correct interpretation is critical to understanding its doctrines.

Does this fully answer our initial question? No. Islam is a complex religion and the Koran (Quran) is a complex book. Many people use its text to vindicate their preconceived notions, as is done with the Bible. One thing is certain however, whatever Muslims advocate would that they all come to the saving knowledge of our Lord and Savior Jesus Christ—the Prince of Peace (Isa. 9:6).

RELIGION & POLITICS

Never discuss religion and politics. Lord help me as I do just that as we approach the next presidential election. Most of my essays discuss positions on biblical topics and suggest a course of action for us as Ministers of the Good News of Jesus Christ. This essay is recounting an ongoing dialog I am having with myself. There are many issues important to the Black community besides the limited issues I am discussing here. I am focusing on only these few to illuminate the rhetorical dilemma I face as a minister of the Gospel and as a black man. As I view the political scene I see issues from several perspectives among them:

> *"Do I vote as a Black man? Do I vote as a minister? Do I vote as a Black minister?"*

As a minister of the Gospel.
As a black man.
As a voter.

As I consider which political candidates to support and what issues inform that choice these perspectives often clash. For example, I would not have had the educational opportunities I had without affirmative action programs extant in the 70's. And I strongly favor the continuance of affirmative action programs for minorities. Therefore it should be clear that I should support political candidates that share this view—ergo the Democrats.

However, I also strongly oppose elective abortion. The senseless killing of millions of unborn children for no reason other than the convenience of the mother is an abomination before the living God (cf. Jer 2:34). I also oppose the homosexual agenda as it seeks to normalize homosexual acts and attempts to get states to sanction homosexual marriage etc.

So I think you see the dilemma. Most candidates that support issues like affirmative action and other issues favorable to our community also support the total liberal agenda including the above mentioned gay and lesbian issues and abortion. So how do I view my responsibility? Do I vote as a Black man? Do I vote as a minister? Do I vote as a Black minister? Do I vote my self-interest and disregard those issues with which I disagree in the interest of what is good for our people—only?

To put it clearly, do I vote for and support Democrat candidates who support the 'Black agenda' such as affirmative action but who also support abortion and the gay and lesbian agenda? One might say: 'Political and moral issues are separate.' Well I am not letting myself off the hook that easily. So here is a question: Would I be willing to give up affirmative action to abolish abortion? Actually I do not believe affirmative action programs are in danger of being eliminated but they are under attack by many Republicans.

I am not suggesting an answer but I am suggesting that as a minister I must consider issues beyond my political self-interest. I at least have to evaluate political candidates holistically. I have to consider the consequences of the political choices I make beyond what helps my personal or community agenda. I must take a stand and here is the stand I take. I am a conservative. I believe that the US Supreme Court's recent decisions in the University of Michigan's affirmative action admissions policies cases in which the court ruled in 2003 to uphold the constitutionality of taking diversity considerations into account in college admissions have settled this matter for the foreseeable future. In other words whoever is elected president and whoever the president appoints to the high court affirmative action will not be appreciably affected. Accordingly I do not feel obligated to vote for a Democrat based on this issue alone.

However the next president will surely have a great impact on court rulings on abortion and the homosexual agenda. Note in this regard the recent Supreme Court decision upholding a national ban on the heinous partial birth abortion procedure. Had not President Bush been in office to appoint conservative judges the court surely would not have ruled in favor of the state ban. The 5-4 ruling said the *Partial_Birth_Abortion_Ban_Act* that Congress passed and President Bush signed into law in 2003 does not violate a woman's constitutional right to an abortion. This is progress.

So I take my stand with the conservatives. This despite their irritating habit of presumptuously pontificating on what is best for African American people. For example when they deride affirmative action they never mention the appalling practice of favoring legacies and development cases in admissions to colleges and universities. (For a discussion of this issue see the next essay The Truth About College Admissions.)

This is a difficult subject for an African American minister of the Gospel. Wherever you stand my brothers and sisters in the ministry, you must take a stand.

2009 Addendum: The above chapter was written several years ago. In 2008 my ideas were put to the test with the candidacy of Barack Obama. I voted for Obama. Why? Because I wanted to. Despite the above discussion when it came down to a choice between Sen. McCain and Sen. Obama I voted for Obama. I could make several arguments in favor of Obama. One of the strongest was his calm consistent approach to the economic crisis contrasted to McCain's wild shifts from day to day.

I thought Obama would make and has made a good president. But what about the other issues abortion and the gay agenda? I put all that aside and voted for Obama—because I just wanted to. I like Obama. I was not going to miss the opportunity to vote for the first viable black candidate for President of this country. And before you say it let me admit: I am a hypocrite! At the time I wrote the first part of this article I never could have conceived of any liberal Democrat that I could ever support for president. But Obama is—what can I say—Obama. And I believe he has done an excellent job especially dealing with the horrific economic emergency he inherited.

So I rightly stand accused of inconsistency and hypocrisy. Well as most sinners say: "But it felt so good!"

THE TRUTH ABOUT COLLEGE ADMISSIONS

As we enter the season when we remember the birthday of Dr. Martin Luther King Jr. it is a good time to discuss a key issue in the Civil Rights Movement: Affirmative Action. Affirmative action has taken many forms from preferences in college admissions to favorable consideration of minority contractors for work with municipalities. My interest here is the current state of affirmative action as it relates to admissions to colleges and universities. Particularly elite colleges, universities and professional schools like medical schools and law schools.

> **"The problem with the debate over affirmative action is that those who support affirmative action are not making the strongest argument."**

Let me interject a couple personal notes. I am a conservative. I vote conservative and support conservative causes and issues. Except for one issue—affirmative action. I support affirmative action in all its manifestations. Whether it is minority recruitment, set asides, diversity or quotas I am for it. I support minority students being given an opportunity to attend the best colleges, universities, law schools etc. Why? Because I was given those opportunities. I started my post high school academic career at Wilson Jr. College. After the Army I went back to school at Kennedy-King Jr. College. While there I did well and two teachers and a counselor mentored me and I was admitted as a transfer student to the College of the University of Chicago. From there I was blessed to get my law degree from the Northwestern University School of Law. My purpose in mentioning these schools is to make the following point: I would not have been admitted to U of C or Northwestern had they not had minority recruitment programs. Simply put, I benefited from affirmative action and I am not about to stop supporting these policies now that I have my paper. That would be hypocrisy.

As I listen to conservative commentators with whom I generally agree it irritates me when they go on and on about affirmative action. Calling it reverse discrimination. It particularly bothers me when African American conservative writers like Thomas Sowell (author of: *Black Rednecks and White Liberals*), Shelby Steele (author of: *White Guilt: How Blacks and Whites Together Destroyed the Promise of the Civil Rights Era*) and Ward Connelly also condemn affirmative action.

Ward Connelly is a black man who spearheaded the fight for the passage of Propositions 209 and 54 in California. Proposition 209 was the initiative that was passed about 10 years ago to get rid of race-based preferences in school admissions, hiring and contracting with municipalities. Proposition 54 would have prevented the state of California from using racial classifications in most of its business. It sought to amend California's Constitution to prohibit state and local governments from using race, ethnicity, color, or national origin to classify current or prospective students, contractors or employees in public education, contracting, or employment operations. Its official title was the "Racial Privacy Initiative." Supporters of the measure said it was the first step towards a "colorblind" society, while opponents felt that it would make it more difficult for the state to provide services and identify and correct racial disparities. Commentators profess that it is only African American students that keep highly qualified white applicants out of America's premier universities. This is a lie.

The problem with the debate over affirmative action is that those who support affirmative action are not making the strongest argument. When we try to support affirmative action we focus on the need to give African American applicants a chance to matriculate to the great schools despite lower academic qualifications as a socially laudable goal. Since minority students often come from primary and secondary schools that do not provide the same quality education as white schools we argue that it is understandable that African American students do not score as well on standardized test like the ACT, GRE or LSAT as white graduates. Therefore the minority student should be given some consideration and special attention in college and grad school admissions.

All this is true and I agree with this position but this is not the strongest argument. Conservatives scoff at this argument. They argue that giving lower qualified minority applicants preferential treatment is unfair and un-American. They say this is unfair to higher qualified white applicants. So the arguments and debates go round and round and the conservatives are winning in court and in the court of public opinion. But there is a dirty little secret these conservatives are keeping that would undermine their positions if supporters of affirmative action knew what was going on.

Here are some important terms we need to become familiar with: "Legacy Preferences" and "Development Cases." These are general terms that apply at all the top schools. There are also some sub terms that are specific to individual schools; they include Harvard's COUR (Committee on University Resources) and Duke University's "Cardboard Box." These last two terms are just particular names for the legacy and development case tradition. I would guess that most supporters of affirmative action never heard these terms and that is why we are not winning the debate. In short all these terms amount to affirmative action for rich white applicants.

What are legacies? They are applicants who are children or grandchildren of alumni. But not just any alumni—rich alumni. Alumni who make substantial contributions to their alma maters. When the children of these generous donors apply to the schools that have received this largesse these children get special consideration and many are admitted with qualifications substantially lower than rejected white applicants who are not related to rich donors.

Development cases. These are applicants who are related to rich potential donors who are not alumni. The parents or grandparents did not attend the school the young people are applying to but they are rich and are potential generous donors—if their children are admitted. There may not be a direct *quid pro quo* but as soon as the applicant is admitted the parent is solicited for contributions by the school.

Why are there Legacy Preferences and Development Cases? MONEY! Schools are obsessed about the state of their endowments. The larger the endowment the better qualified faculty they can hire. The better the library. And generally the more sound the schools financial foundation. This is particularly important in these times of shrinking federal assistance to colleges and universities. An important part of a university president's legacy is how the school's endowment increased during his or her tenure. So a less qualified even a far less qualified student who is the son or daughter of rich alumni will be given preference over a highly qualified applicant with no familial connection to the school. Also the children of prominent politicians also receive favorable treatment lower qualifications notwithstanding. This is the way it is. But it is a well guarded secret.

So lets take an example. Consider a white male applicant to Harvard's undergraduate school. He has an excellent high school record and graduated at the top of his prep school class. He was editor of the school paper and president of the senior class. He was high school valedictorian and had a perfect SAT score. He applies assuming he will be admitted. But he receives a letter informing him that he has not been admitted. He does some research and finds out that five minority students with lower academic records and SAT scores were admitted under the schools diversity program. He runs to federal court suing the school charging that the minority students are the reason he was not admitted. No mention is made of the (for example) 89 whites with lower qualifications that were also admitted. The white legacies and development cases that were given preferential treatment over him are not mentioned in his "reverse discrimination" suit. No—it is the five African American students that prevented him from being admitted. It is that African American female that is sitting in his seat not any of the 89 unqualified whites with family and financial ties to the school who took his place.

When I was in law school Dean James A. Rahl told my classmate and friend Wilbert Allen that 75% of the students at Northwestern's law school were related to alumni. 75% legacies! But all the law suits like Regents of the University of California v. Bakke *and* DeFunis *that were so important at the time focused on minority students not rich majority students that were given preferential treatment in admissions. For example in the landmark* Bakke *case the US Supreme Court held that race could be one of the factors considered in choosing a diverse student body in university admissions decisions. However, that the use of quotas in such affirmative action programs was not permissible. Thus the University of California, Davis, and Medical School had, by maintaining a 16% minority quota, discriminated against Allan Bakke a white applicant. Bakke had twice been rejected by the medical school, even though he had a higher grade point average than a number of minority candidates who were admitted. However there is no doubt there were more white legacies with lower grade point averages or test scores than Bakke that were admitted but Bakke did not claim that admission of these lower qualified legacies violated his rights. No—it was only the admission of the minority students that violated his rights.*

This was also the case in another important decision: DeFunis versus Odegaard and the University of Washington. *In that case Marco DeFunis, Jr. was denied admission as a first-year student at the University of Washington Law School and sued the school on reverse discrimination grounds and the court ordered the school to admit him. I am sure there were whites students admitted with lower qualifications than DeFunis but it was the few African American students he claimed were responsible for him not being admitted—not the less qualified white legacies.*

Legacies and development cases are routinely admitted to American's finest universities over white applicants with superior academic records and test scores. But no one talks about this 'discrimination' in favor of the rich. "Whether one is for or against affirmative action, it is important to frame the issue in context. Even as conservative critics paint affirmative action for college-bound minorities as giving African Americans, Hispanics, and Native Americans an unfair advantage over more capable white candidates, the truth is the reverse. The number of whites enjoying preference far outweighs the number of minorities," (Daniel Golden, *The Price Of Admission—How America's Ruling Class Buys It's Way into Elite Colleges—and Who Gets Left Outside the Gates* (New York: Crown Publishers, 2006), 6.)

Believe Rush Limbaugh, Laura Ingraham and Ann Coulter (all of whom I enjoy listening to and reading) know about these practices but they focus their ire on the miniscule number of minority students admitted to schools under diversity programs to the exclusion of any mention of the preferences given to rich legacies and development cases. Our 'leaders' never mention this situation when trying to defend affirmative action programs. As the bible says: *"My people are destroyed for lack of knowledge . . . ."* (Hos. 4:6) We are in tough times for the movement toward minority advancement. Many of our 'leaders' have been undermined by critics and their own failings. The African American community is particularly bereft of defenders during this time of conservative ascendancy. We need to gird our children with knowledge and wisdom and a vision for their futures for *"Where there is no vision, the people perish . . . ."* (Prov. 29:18)

TELLING THE TRUTH— THE LAST SIN

(Postmodernism and the Minister)

In olden days, a glimpse of stocking
Was looked on as something shocking.
But now, God knows,
—Anything goes.
Good authors too who once knew better words
Now only use four-letter words
Writing prose.
—Anything goes
The world has gone mad today
And good's bad today,
And black's white today,
And day's night today,
(*Anything Goes* By Cole Porter—1934)

    This song was a hit in 1934. The words to this song could have been written yesterday. It is certainly true that today anything goes. All manner of unrighteousness is winked at (Act 17:30) and excused. There is however, something new in the air about the sinfulness of our times. Now the sentiments expressed in this song would be labeled "intolerant." To be labeled intolerant is the worse thing you can be called by the world today. Intolerant! To be called intolerant means you are narrow-minded. You are homophobic if you are against gay "marriage." Racist if you suggest that the high illegitimacy rate in our community is undesirable. Sexist if you are pro life. Anti-Semitic if you present the Gospel of Jesus Christ to Jewish people. And on and on it goes.

The very language used by the media and the interest groups they generally support is slanted toward thwarting and intimidating Christians into not standing for righteousness or telling the truth. This social phenomenon has a name—Postmodernism. In a postmodern society there is no absolute truth. Such as "Jesus Christ is Lord." There are no controlling rules or norms for society. Not even God has the right to say what is right and wrong. Why? Because what is wrong for you may not be wrong for me and you

> "One survey found that 62% of "born-again Christians" say they don't believe in the existence of absolute truth."

have no right to call what I do wrong. Solomon spoke of a society like this when he said: "This is the way of an adulteress: She eats and wipes her mouth and says, 'I've done nothing wrong." (Prov. 30:20 NIV)

In our postmodern society truth is relative. No one has the right to condemn or judge anybody for anything. No matter how heinous the act or crime someone will defend it, e.g. Partial birth abortion. The Boy Scouts have no right to refuse to hire homosexual scoutmasters. That is intolerant. The Christian has no right to say that Jesus is the only way to be saved. That is intolerant.

After all didn't Jesus say "Judge not, that ye be not judged"? (Matt. 7:1) Yes Jesus surely said these words. But Jesus was not saying do not judge sin for He went on to say: "For with what judgment ye judge, ye shall be judged: and with what measure ye mete, it shall be measured to you again. And why beholdest thou the mote that is in thy brother's eye, but considerest not the beam that is in thine own eye? Or how wilt thou say to thy brother, Let me pull out the mote out of thine eye; and, behold, a beam is in thine own eye? Thou hypocrite, first cast out the beam out of thine own eye; and then shalt thou see clearly to cast out the mote out of thy brother's eye." (Matt. 7:2-5)

Jesus is not saying do not judge. Jesus is saying do not be a hypocrite when you judge. Jesus is saying make sure that sin in your life is not clouding your judgment of others. Jesus is telling us how to judge and what standard to apply. If Christians who have the Holy Spirit are not qualified to censure sin—who is? What saith the scriptures? "Do ye not know that the saints shall judge the world? And if the world shall be judged by you, are ye unworthy to judge the smallest matters? Know ye not that we shall judge angels? How much more things that pertain to this life?" (1 Cor. 6:2-3)

How are we to be salt and light (Matt. 5:13-16) if we take no positions on the wrongs we see all around us. For example if Christians do not speak out against abortion who will? We are to speak our truth with grace, seasoned with salt, that we may know how we ought to answer every man. (Col. 4:6) But we are to answer when confronted with injustice, unrighteousness and sin. Imagine a world without the church of Christ (as will be the case immediately after the rapture). For centuries it has been the church that has stood steadfastly against all manner of evil in the world. It is Christians that have ameliorated injustice and suffering throughout the world. Who sends missionaries to feed, clothe and provide medical care to millions of starving suffering people throughout the world? Not the ACLU or even the NAACP. No it is the church.

But how many times have we heard fellow Christians quote the "judge not" verse just like the sinners do. One survey found that 62 percent of "born-again Christians say they don't believe in the existence of absolute truth." (*Preaching to a Postmodern World* by Graham Johnson, p. 16) Even Christians have been intimidated by the sinner's question: "Who are you to judge?"

As saints of God and as ministers of the Gospel we must stand for the truth of the Gospel message and against all unrighteousness. What God prohibits as we interact with our "brother" or fellow Christians is condemnation. We are not to condemn our brother in Christ. Why? Because "There is therefore now no condemnation to them which are in Christ Jesus," (Rom 8:1a) Condemnation is the providence of God alone. But standing against injustice, unrighteousness and wrong is our calling. The bible never retreats from calling sins by their proper names. (See: 1 Cor. 6:9, 10; Gal. 5:19-21; 2 Cor. 12:21 etc.)

So what is the last sin in this postmodern age? What is the only sin that society acknowledges? Indeed what is the last and only sin that our society universally condemns? What is the sin that all in our society are willing to stand against and denounce? It is a sin that all Christians should be guilty of committing. It is THE SIN OF CALLING SIN—**SIN**!

RACISM—WHAT DIFFERENCE DOES IT MAKE?

In law school I remember a case that had the following facts. A man fell from a 50 story roof. On the way down he was shot. The issue: of what crime should the shooter be charged? The man was already falling to his death when he was shot. So what role did the bullet pay in his unfortunate end. My people are like the falling man. Black people are doing themselves so much damage that it is difficult to determine what role racism and discrimination continues to play in our lives.

School—If our black young people do not have the sense to see that staying in school where they get a free education (albeit not the best in some public schools—more on that later) then what role does discrimination in hiring for jobs and housing play? Can a young black person blame racism and discrimination for their lack of opportunities when they voluntarily dropped out of high school.

> "She was critical of the appalling out of wedlock birthrate among black women."

Family—Recently there was demonstration in Washington DC where many black "leaders" spoke. The usual ones, Jesse Jackson, Al Shaprton, Louis Farrakhan, Harry Belafonte etc. These speakers condemned racism by white America as they usually do and not without justification. These speakers were greeted by loud applause at all the usual points in their speeches. Then from out of the blue an African American woman spoke about the lack of stability in the black family. She criticized some black men for rampant unfaithfulness to their wives and sexual promiscuity. She was critical of the appalling out of wedlock birthrate among black women. She had the audacity to suggest that the lack of family stability was causing economic deprivation in our community.

All these points were met by stony silence from the crowd. Nobody clapped. The gathering did not want to hear anything about our problems. Nobody wanted to hear what we could do as a people to ameliorate the affects of racism on our community. I would not have been surprised if she were booed off the podium. All they wanted was what the white man was doing to us.

Politics—Those of us who grew up in Chicago have faced countless elections where the name Daley was on the ballot. Either the father or the son. While our "leaders" criticize the Daley Machine and the plantation politics of the Daley administrations I guarantee all Daley has to worry about in any future election is a possible black candidate in the Primary elections. Because if Daley is on the ballot in the general election I don't care who the republican candidate is African American's will vote for Daley because he is a Democrat. Our people (exclude me because I have never voted for any Daley) will vote democratic no matter what.

Religion, Ethics, Politics—African American evangelical born again Christians vote for Democrat candidates no matter what positions they take on abortion and the gay and lesbian agenda. Black ministers say that 'Political and moral issues are separate.' That is ridiculous. Moral issues are not separate from anything. The moral issues come first. We are Christians! But that does not mean anything to black Christians when it comes to supporting democrat candidates that support everything that we say we abhor.

Clearly we have no problem with abortion, euthanasia, the homosexual agenda etc. If we did those problems would manifest themselves in walking it like we talk it. Whenever I raise these issues with black Christians and ministers their eyes glaze over and they start talking about how low down President Bush is. Bush hates black people! They have no empirical data to back this up they just hate him. They are completely in line with white Democrats who hate Bush for taking the kinds of moral stands we black Christian and ministers are supposed to support. But white Democrats have told black people to hate Bush and black people obey. And it is of no consequences that our president is a Christian. I even heard a minister criticize Bush's Christianity because he is a Southern Baptist. I never heard that criticism of Jimmy Carter!

School Vouchers—as mentioned above many public schools may not provide the best educational foundation for black young people. But white democrats have told black people to oppose school vouchers that would give black students the opportunity to attend schools that would provide such a foundation. So now what? This does not make sense. White Democrats have dictated an agenda of depravity, death, abortion, perpetual inferior education etc. and we African Americans just follow their "leadership" down the road to continued depravity and disadvantageous policies.

Music—Why is R. Kelley a star in the African American community? This is a man accused of urinating on a teenage black girl! Many of the words to black hip hop 'music' are disgraceful. No one is imposing any of this on our community we are willingly participating in self destructive self loathing behavior. I hear young girls walking home from a black high school close to my home calling each other "bitch" like young black women used to call each other "girl." As in "girl let me tell you . . ." Now it's "bitch where you going." This is unspeakable. It is beyond words how low we have sunk.

Crime—I heard Angela Davis speak a few years ago and she decried the expansion of the prison industry and it's affect on the black community—black men in particular. She is right but who are all these black men in prison for committing crimes against. OTHER BLACK PEOPLE! The vast majority of black men in prison are not there accused of hurting white people. No, black convicts are there for alleged crimes against other black people. Black criminals generally do not commit crimes against white people. And of course it is anathema to snitch and help the police capture these criminals victimizing our community. So how much sympathy am I to have about this army of black criminals preying on our community? I am not talking about innocent black men behind bars who did not have access to the kind of legal representation OJ had. Surely if OJ had the kind of representation most black defendants have he would have been convicted.

So what role does racism play in this mess? I heard a black man refer to Dr. Condoleezza Rice in a derogatory sexual distortion of her name. Think about that! To denigrate one of the most outstanding black women in the world in such a manner. Rather than appreciate the accomplishments and excellence of Dr. Rice and Colin Powel and other blacks of achievement in the Bush administration black people in the public eye insult and disrespect people we should hold up as examples to our young people. But no, their heroes are 50 cent, Ditty and Rob Kelley. What a mess!

So as we fall to our deaths what difference does it make if white people shot us. We are headed for destruction anyway and we jumped off the building.

DID JEPHTHAH KILL HIS DAUGHTER?

What shall we make of Jephthah? A man the bible suggests killed his daughter to keep a vow to the Lord who commanded Israel not to do that very thing. (Deut. 12:31, 32; 18:10-12) Let's look at what Jephthah said and then see if we can figure out what he did.

> *"And Jephthah vowed a vow unto the LORD, and said, If thou shalt without fail deliver the children of Ammon into mine hands, Then it shall be, that whatsoever cometh forth of the doors of my house to meet me, when I return in peace from the children of Ammon, shall surely be the LORD's, and I will offer it up for a burnt offering." And Jephthah came to Mizpeh unto his house, and, behold, his daughter came out to meet him with timbrels and with dances: and she was his only child; beside her he had neither son nor daughter.*
>
> *And it came to pass, when he saw her, that he rent his clothes, and said, Alas, my daughter! thou hast brought me very low, and thou art one of them that trouble me: for I have opened my mouth unto the LORD, and I cannot go back.*
>
> *And she said unto him, My father, if thou hast opened thy mouth unto the LORD, do to me according to that which hath proceeded out of thy mouth; forasmuch as the LORD hath taken vengeance for thee of thine enemies, even of the children of Ammon.*
>
> *37 And she said unto her father, Let this thing be done for me: let me alone two months, that I may go up and down upon the mountains, and bewail my virginity, I and my fellows.*
>
> *And he said, Go. And he sent her away for two months: and she went with her companions, and bewailed her virginity upon the mountains.*

And it came to pass at the end of two months, that she returned
unto her father, who did with her according to his vow which he had
vowed: and she knew no man. And it was a custom in Israel,
That the daughters of Israel went yearly to lament the daughter
of Jephthah the Gileadite four days in a year." (Judg. 11:40)

What a mess! Jephthah appears to have committed to killing his daughter because of the vow he made to the Lord. Did Jephthah indeed kill his daughter in the Lord's name? After all does not the scripture say: "If a man vow a vow unto the LORD, or swear an oath to bind his soul with a bond; he shall not break his word, he shall do according to all that proceedeth out of his mouth." (Num 30:2) Thus Jephthah was bound to carry out the terms of the vow.

But what were the terms of this vow? Many articles and commentaries have been written examining this difficult passage. I will discuss just a couple approaches. Some scholars break this vow into two parts to be applied under two circumstances. Namely if a person is first to meet him that person *"shall surely be the LORD's."* That person shall be dedicated to a life of celibate service to the Lord. As one set apart for tabernacle service (cf. Exod. 38:8; 1 Sam. 2:22)

Thus she would never become a mother resulting in the extinction of Jephthah's line, since she was his only child (Archer: Encyclopedia *of Bible Difficulties,* p. 165) Note that his daughter asked her father for two months to "bewail my virginity" not to morn her impending death. If she was about to die I don't think being a virgin would be equal to being on the bewailment list.

Note that Jephthah says "whatsoever cometh forth of the doors of my house." Not, whosoever. This allowed for a person or an animal. This leads to the second part of the vow. "I will offer it up for a burnt offering" He says he will offer "it" not him or her for a burnt offering. So this could be an animal. OK but what about the connecting word "and" between the two parts of the vow. That is hard. One of my seminary teachers said that a better translation of this text uses the word "or" rather than "and." So the vow would be to either dedicate a human to serving the Lord OR sacrifice an animal as a burnt offering.

One thing is sure God abhors human sacrifice. *"Thou shalt not do so unto the LORD thy God: for every abomination to the LORD, which he hateth, have they done unto their gods; for even their sons and their daughters they have burnt in the fire to their gods."* (Deut 12:31) "There shall not be found among you any one that maketh his son or his daughter to pass through the fire, or that useth divination, or an observer of times, or an enchanter, or a witch," (Deut 18:10)

In the light of these verses, one thing is sure. Jephthah did not kill his daughter. Why am I so sure? Had Jephthah committed such an abominable act as murdering his own daughter he would not be listed as one of the heroes of faith in Hebrews 11:32 along with the likes of Samuel, Samson and David. No, I believe that Jephthah and his daughter will be available for an interview on the subject—in heaven. If he killed her, she might be there but I don't think he would.

In any case Jephthah could have been relieved of his vow by making the payment outlined in the Law to wit: fifty shekels of silver.

> *"And the LORD spake unto Moses, saying, Speak unto the children of Israel, and say unto them, When a man shall make a singular vow, the persons shall be for the LORD by thy estimation. And thy estimation shall be of the male from twenty years old even unto sixty years old, even thy estimation shall be fifty shekels of silver, after the shekel of the sanctuary. And if it be a female, then thy estimation shall be thirty shekels."* (Lev 27:1-4)

ELECTION—IS GOD UNFAIR?

Election and predestination to the world and too many Christians these concepts seem unfair. It is unfair for God to predestine to save some and not others. If the choice of who is saved is under the sovereign control of God and man has no effect of God's choice of who is ultimately saved then it is unfair to the lost since they are helpless to choose salvation or damnation.

What about the poor lost soul that would have come to God if God had allowed him to come. The logic of these complaints against God seem at first glance sound. However let's look a little closer at man's condition and God's sovereignty. The bible describes mans condition thus:

> **"He would be just in allowing all man-kind to go to hell."**

Rom 3:23
>> *For all have sinned, and come short of the glory of God;*

Rom 5:12
>> *Wherefore, as by one man sin entered into the world, and death by sin; and so death passed upon all men, for that all have sinned:*

Ps 14:3
>> *They are all gone aside, they are all together become filthy: there is none that doeth good, no, not one.*

Ps 53:3
>> *Every one of them is gone back: they are altogether become filthy; there is none that doeth good, no, not one.*

Rom 3:10
>> *As it is written, There is none righteous, no, not one:*

Rom 3:12
> *They are all gone out of the way, they are together become unprofitable; there is none that doeth good, no, not one.*

So if there are none that deserve salvation none have a right to demand salvation. That is if all men deserve judgment no man in the history of mankind from Adam till the end of the world has a right to salvation. So if God decided not to save anybody He would be just in allowing all mankind to go to hell. No charge of unfairness could be lodged against God if all men were lost.

However, let us say that God in His sovereignty chose to save only one man or woman in all the history of mankind. ONLY ONE! Would that not reflect infinite grace and mercy toward that one person? Yes. If only one person in history were saved God would be showing infinite mercy. And it would have required the death, burial and resurrection of our Lord to effectuate that one person's salvation.

So the fact that God in His infinite grace and mercy chooses to save millions of lost hell bound souls including you and I should cause us to fall on our faces in worship and praise and thanks to the almighty God who chose us for no reason than that He set his love on us. God so loved Richard C. Anderson that he gave His only begotten Son that whosoever (that is whosoever He chooses to call and regenerate) believes on Him should not parish but have eternal life.

So there is no charge of unfairness, on the contrary God is beyond fair He is loving, kind, gracious and forgiving to choose to save even one of us undeserving sinners from the eternal punishment we deserve.

ENDING WELL

This essay may seem a little preachy or didactic, but that is because I am writing to myself more than others. It takes a lifetime to build a reputation but only minutes to lose it all to scandal and disgrace. I think about this subject from time to time and it always leads me to pray: "Lord help me to end well." We all love being ministers. We love having a personal intimate relationship with Jesus. We are called to certain ministries and carrying them out is our main activity in life. We all look forward to going on with Christ and moving "up" in ministry—whatever that may mean in our individual callings. We know most of us will not be a TD Jakes or Paula White but we want to be all that God would have us to be. We want to go on with with God and have productive careers in ministry.

But what about the end. Going on with the Lord requires staying on a very narrow path. It requires resisting the temptations Satan places in our path to derail our witness and ministry. Satan cannot keep us out of heaven. We are secure in our salvation so he tries to destroy any positive influence we may have as ministers of the Gospel. Simply put Satan wants to cause us to sin and thus ruin our reputation and ministry. Satan takes great glee in a fallen minister. Satan loves it when a minister is involved in scandal. And those of us who are not famous are still the targets of his attempts to ruin our reputation. Reputations we have built up over years can be destroyed in an instant.

> **"But he told Balak to send the women of his country in among the Israelites to seduce them. . . "**

SAMSON

Think of Samson. A man set apart for service to God. "*. . . and no razor shall come on his head: for the child shall be a Nazarite unto God from the womb: and he shall begin to deliver Israel out of the hand of the Philistines.*

(Judg. 13:5) Samson had enormous strength and he had the Holy Spirit. (Judg. 13:15) He had everything going for him but because of his weakness for foreign women he ended badly. And of Solomon the wise giver of proverbs in the bible says: *"But king Solomon loved many strange women, Of the nations concerning which the LORD said unto the children of Israel, Ye shall not go in to them, neither shall they come in unto you: for surely they will turn away your heart after their gods: Solomon clave unto these in love . . . . when Solomon was old, that his wives turned away his heart after other gods: and his heart was not perfect with the LORD his God . . . And Solomon did evil in the sight of the LORD . . . And the LORD was angry with Solomon."* (1 Kings 11:1-9) Note that Solomon's sin occurred when he was old. Solomon did not end well.

BALAAM AND BALAK

Consider the story of Balaam and Balak. This is a long story with parts of it told in various Old and New Testament scriptures. (e.g.: Numbers 22; 23; 31; Jude 11; 2 Peter 2 and Revelation 2; Deut 11 etc.) The essence of the story is this. Balak hired Balaam to curse Israel who he feared would defeat him in war. Balak could not curse Israel because God had blessed Israel. And we know: *"The blessing of the LORD, it maketh rich, and he addeth no sorrow with it"*. (Prov. 10:22) So Balaam could not curse God's people. But he told Balak to send the women of his country in among the Israelites to seduce them and cause them to forsake their God. And sure enough the men of Israel were seduced by these women leading to sin, idolatry and eventually terrible chastisement by God. (Num 25) So what Satan could not curse he corrupted with idolatry and immorality. So God added no sorrow with His blessing but Satan caused the men of Israel to bring sorrow on themselves and many innocent people.

ISRAEL UNDER THE BLESSING AND PROTECTION

Here was Israel under the blessing and protection of God and they bring on themselves the downfall that Satan could not cause by himself. And like Israel God is saying to us: *"Behold, I set before you this day a blessing and a curse; A blessing, if ye obey the commandments of the LORD your God, which I command you this day: And a curse, if ye will not obey the commandments of the LORD your God, but turn aside out of the way which I command you this day, to go after other gods, which ye have not known."* (Deut 11:26-28) We all have weak points. There are areas in our lives where we are vulnerable to satanic attack and temptation. We know what they are and so does the devil. His goal is to cause us to end badly. He is trying to make us dishonor the name of Christ and our church. He wants to tear up our families and ruin our lives. These are strong words but this is the war we are in. We are in a hard, deadly struggle with our enemy and we cannot let our guard down for even a moment. And when I say we, I mean me.

INNOCENT VICTIMS

Satan's attempt to destroy our ministry is not limited to causing us to sin. We could be the innocent victims of a smear attack, a rumor falsely spread or a false charge by the police. Several months ago I was stopped by the police for a "rolling stop at a stop sign." While waiting for my ticket I noticed that there were four police cars behind me and several officers including a high ranking (white shirt and gold on his cap) supervisor talking to the officer who initially pulled me over. They were looking at my papers and looking at my car. I got on my cell phone and called my lawyer and my wife and they were on their way to the scene. After almost an hour sitting in my car the policeman finally gave me the ticket. I ask him (very politely) what took so long and he said there was some question about my AAA card. To this day I don't know what was really going on. But that is an example of how fast a situation can go bad.

HEDGE

God has a hedge about us and Satan cannot take it down. (Job 1:10) But we can weaken it from the inside. Satan cannot get inside our wall of protection but he is outside calling us to come out and play. I recently heard a song that said "don't let Satan ride in your car he will end up driving." And he will take you farther than you want to go; keep you longer than you want to stay and cost you more than you want to pay. God has called each of us to a unique service in building His kingdom. Let's get before the Lord and renew our commitment to persevere faithfully and end well that we might say: "*I have fought a good fight, I have finished my course, I have kept the faith.*" (2 Tim 4:7)

FAITH—THE GIFT OF SIGHT

"For by grace are ye saved through faith; and that not of yourselves: it is the gift of God:" (Eph 2:8) Let us focus on the gift aspect of faith. Faith is a gift of God. We do not have faith because we reason out our situation and decide from what we see that God is faithful. No God gives us the ability to believe and trust in Him. We can't have faith in God till God comes into our hearts by regeneration. I think most Christians believe that first we have faith and then God rewards that faith by coming into our hearts. But if He has not already changed our hearts we will not and indeed cannot have faith in Him.

> *"God is telling Isaiah to prophecy to people who will not hear or understand the prophesy."*

So what is this gift? We all know the definition of faith: *"Now faith is the substance of things hoped for, the evidence of things not seen."* (Heb 11:1) Let us focus on "things unseen." One of Jesus' favorite expressions was: *"He that hath ears to hear, let him hear."* (Matt 13:15; 43; Mark 4:9; 23; 7:16; Lk. 8:8; 14:35; Rev 2:11, 17, 29; 3:6, 13, 22) This expression related to a prophecy in Isaiah: *"And he said, Go, and tell this people, Hear ye indeed, but understand not; and see ye indeed, but perceive not. Make the heart of this people fat, and make their ears heavy, and shut their eyes; lest they see with their eyes, and hear with their ears, and understand with their heart, and convert, and be healed."* (Isa. 6:9-10) God is telling Isaiah to prophesy to people who will not hear or understand the prophesy.

What saith Jeremiah? *"Hear now this, O foolish people, and without understanding; which have eyes, and see not; which have ears, and hear not:"* (Jer. 5:21)

What saith Ezekiel? *"Son of man, thou dwellest in the midst of a rebellious house, which have eyes to see, and see not; they have ears to hear, and hear not: for they are a rebellious house."* (Ezek 12:2)

What saith Dr. Luke? *"Saying, Go unto this people, and say, Hearing ye shall hear, and shall not understand; and seeing ye shall see, and not perceive: For the heart of this people is waxed gross, and their ears are dull of hearing, and their eyes have they closed; lest they should see with their eyes, and hear with their ears, and understand with their heart, and should be converted, and I should heal them. Be it known therefore unto you, that the salvation of God is sent unto the Gentiles, and that they will hear it."* (Acts 28:26-28)

What saith Paul? *"(According as it is written, God hath given them the spirit of slumber, eyes that they should not see, and ears that they should not hear;) unto this day."* (Rom 11:8)

There is much theology in these scriptures but let's focus on one aspect. The ability to trust the evidence of things unseen is a gift of God. Over the centuries God has given and withheld this gift to people during various dispensations to bring about His purposes in the earth. God has allowed the church the body of Christ to see, hear, understand and trust in His word and spiritual realities. Until God opens our eyes we cannot see to trust. Until God opens our ears we cannot hear. Does not faith come by hearing? (Rom 10:17) But if God does not open our ears we cannot respond in faith. Lydia was a great woman in scripture but first God opened her heart then only then did she attend *"unto the things which were spoken of Paul."* (Acts 16:14) Notice her heart first had to be opened by the Lord so that she could respond to the Gospel presented by Paul.

Consider Elisha's servant. When the army of the king of Syria came to take Elisha into custody his servant was sore afraid. But *". . . Elisha prayed, and said, LORD, I pray thee, open his eyes, that he may see. And the LORD opened the eyes of the young man; and he saw: and, behold, the mountain was full of horses and chariots of fire round about Elisha."* (2 Kings 6:17) Note the chariots of fire were there all along but the servant's physical eyes had to be opened into the spiritual world for him to have faith in the army of the Lord. That army of the Lord was there before he saw them. Likewise the truths that we hold on to by faith were already there and true before we trusted. Faith is when God enables us to see into and manifest in the physical realm what is already true in the spiritual realm. (Andrew Wommack "The Reality of Faith")

If we are blessed in the spiritual world we are blessed in the natural. This applies to healing, prosperity, provisions, protection and countless other aspects of our lives. God provides for us in the sprit all we need in the natural. As Bishop Arthur M. Brazier said God has given him a job to do and God will allow him to do it. God has made all provision necessary for him to complete the work assigned to him. What we see in the natural God had already provided for in the spiritual. And in the natural Bishop Brazier will continue to "*. . . guard everything within the limits of my post and quit my post only when properly relieved.*" (US Army 1ˢᵗ General Order)

Our faith is not a process of mental analysis of the known facts of the gospel. Most of the western world knows the facts of the gospel of Christ. But what has not happened to the unsaved is that their hearts have not been opened so that they can hear with their spiritual ears and see with spiritual eyes the truth of the saving grace of Jesus Christ.

Why does one person you witness to or bring to church respond in faith and others do not? They all hear the same preaching and see the same things but only some have been granted the gift of faith and hear the call of God (Matt 8:13) while others sit and hear "foolishness." (1 Cor. 1:18) Oh what a matchless gift this faith that we rest upon. That we walk on and in. Indeed the just shall live by faith. (Hab. 2:4; Rom 1:17; Gal 3:11; Heb 10:38) We have been given the greatest gift of all. Grace through faith in Jesus Christ. We should weep. We should fall down and worship and praise and thank God for granting us the gift of having faith in Him; for opening our eyes and unstopping our ears. Because without Him we would neither hear nor see His mighty works.

FORGIVENESS—DO THE RIGHT THING

God does not forgive sin! Every sin that has ever been committed or ever will be committed by man is punished. The wages of sin is death. (Rom 6:23) For every sin committed someone must pay—either the sinner or Jesus. God's justice demands that no sin goes unpunished. So God does not forgive SIN, He forgives SINNERS. But what a terrible price Jesus paid for my forgiveness. Therefore I should not take God's forgiveness for granted. Nor should I take my brother's forgiveness for granted. Forgiveness is a precious thing. I must not wrong my brother and act like nothing happened while he or she is left to forgive me. When I injure or offend my brother in Christ I *must* go to him and repent and ask for forgiveness. I must repent *before* he is obligated to forgive me.

> *"We have should stop placing the entire obligation for reconciliation on the aggrieved people in the church."*

However, before I take up the general topic of forgiveness lets look at how some biblical luminaries have responded to being wronged. King Zedekiah had Jeremiah flogged, imprisoned and thrown into a muddy dungeon. (Jer. 38:6) If Ebed-melech the Ethiopian had not rescued him he would have died. Here is what Jeremiah asks God to do to his enemies. (Emphasis mine)

"Render unto them a recompence, O LORD, according to the work of their hands. Give them sorrow of heart, thy curse unto them. Persecute and destroy them in anger from under the heavens of the LORD." (Lam 3:62-66) This sounds more like David than the "weeping prophet." Take a look at Jeremiah 52:8-11 to see the terrible end of Zedekiah.

Here is what David asks God to do to an enemy of his: *"Set thou a wicked man over him: and let Satan stand at his right hand . . . let him be condemned . . .*

Let his days be few . . . Let his children be fatherless, and his wife a widow . . . Let his children be continually vagabonds, and beg . . . Let the extortioner catch all that he hath; and let the strangers spoil his labour . . . Let there be none to extend mercy unto him: neither let there be any to favour his fatherless children . . . Let this be the reward of mine adversaries from the LORD, and of them that speak evil against my soul." (Verses from Psalms 109)

Those are imprecatory prayers from the Old Testament and not everything described is recommended or approved. But along with loving your enemies, blessing them that curse you and doing good to them that hate you, and praying for them which despitefully use you and persecute you (Matt 5:44) you may also react as Paul who told Timothy: *"Alexander the coppersmith did me much evil: the Lord reward him according to his works: Of whom be thou ware also; for he hath greatly withstood our words."* (2Tim 4:14-15) In other words Paul asks God to punish him and told Timothy not to trust him.

Sermons on forgiveness usually focus on the obligations of the person wronged. Favorite scriptures cited are: *"And when ye stand praying, forgive, if ye have ought against any: that your Father also which is in heaven may forgive you your trespasses. But if ye do not forgive, neither will your Father which is in heaven forgive your trespasses."* (Mark 11:25-26). And *"Then came Peter to him, and said, Lord, how oft shall my brother sin against me, and I forgive him? till seven times? Jesus saith unto him, I say not unto thee, Until seven times: but, Until seventy times seven."* (Matt 18:21-22).

These are wonderful verses and our Lord's instructions are clear concerning our obligation to forgive our brothers and sisters in Christ repeatedly. But that is not all Jesus said about forgiveness. Jesus not only placed obligations on the harmed brother He also had placed some conditions on forgiveness. Jesus said: *"Take heed to yourselves: If thy brother trespass against thee, rebuke him; and if he repent, forgive him. And if he trespass against thee seven times in a day, and seven times in a day turn again to thee, saying, I repent; thou shalt forgive him."* (Luke 17:3-4).

Jesus said if a fellow Christian ("brother") trespasses against you "REBUKE HIM" and "IF HE REPENT" forgive him! It is true that the wronged brother must forgive the person who offended him but that obligation attaches *after* the offender repents and ask for forgiveness. *"If he repent, forgive him."* Consider these verses: *"Therefore if thou bring thy gift to the altar, and there rememberest that thy brother hath ought against thee; Leave there thy gift before the altar, and go thy way; first be reconciled to thy brother, and then come and offer thy gift."* (Matt 5:23-24). Note Jesus did not say that if you remember you have something against your brother. No he said if you remember he has "OUGHT AGAINST THEE." That is if you remember that you have done something against your brother YOU go to him and reconcile (repent). Make it right then come back and offer your gift.

We should stop placing the entire obligation for reconciliation on the aggrieved people in the church. Furthermore there is no substitute for repentance. Too often we offend someone and rather than go to that person and apologize we indirectly do something nice for them. We treat them nice—for a while. That is not repentance. Go to your brother or sister look him or her in the eye and say "I am sorry for what I did. I was wrong please forgive me." And do not say: "I'm sorry *IF* I offended you." That is a hypothetical apology. That says what I did was not wrong but you took it wrong. That is not repentance. I know when I'm wrong and I must face it and repent.

Why is this so important? We Christians get enough opposition from the world, the flesh and the Devil; we do not need to add to one another's burdens. We should always seek to help one another. "*A new commandment I give unto you, That ye love one another; as I have loved you, that ye also love one another. By this shall all men know that ye are my disciples, if ye have love one to another.*" (John 13:34-35) We are recognized as Disciples of Christ by how we treat each other.

Remember God hates anyone who "*soweth discord among brethren.*" (Proverbs 6:16-19). It is a serious matter to offend God's children. Jesus said: "*But whoso shall offend one of these little ones which believe in me, it were better for him that a millstone were hanged about his neck, and that he were drowned in the depth of the sea . . . woe to that man by whom the offence cometh!*" (Matt 18:6-7) We will also answer for our treatment of one another at the judgment seat of Christ where every idle word and deed will be judged. (Rom 14:10; 2 Cor. 5:10)

So what should the offended party do? Give the situation to God. If the person who has wronged you is not saved pray that they get saved. That is a very powerful prayer and God may be using you to show that person Jesus and His love. If the person is a Christian also give the situation to God. Pray for the strength to love that person. Don't let your anger eat at you. "*Be ye angry, and sin not: let not the sun go down upon your wrath.*" (Eph 4:26) God will sort the situation out. (Rom 12:19)

I don't ever want my disappointment to cause me to sin against any of God's people. I love God but I also fear Him. Job said: "*What then shall*

I do when God riseth up? and when he visiteth, what shall I answer him?"
(Job 31:14) My point is this. It is sinful and dangerous to harm a child of
God. God does not like it and the person in the wrong should seek out the
offended Christian and repent—fast! Because the bible says: "shall not God
avenge his own elect . . ." (Luke 18:7) *"Seeing it is a righteous thing with God
to recompense tribulation to them that trouble you;"* (2 Thess. 1:6)

FROM HEROD TO PILATE

Herod the Great and Pontius Pilate are two central figures in the bible story of God's plan of redemption for mankind. Herod was called "The Great" not for any great work or attribute but because he was the eldest son of Antipater. Herod put down any opposition to Roman rule and maintained order among the Jewish people of Judea. He slaughtered all male infants who could possibly be considered threats to his throne as king of Judea. Even his wife Mariamne became a victim of his suspicion and brutality. One of his greatest accomplishments was building the Temple in Jerusalem which gained him favor among the Jews.

> "... have you ever wondered why Hebrew women considered it a curse not to be able have children?"

Jesus was born in Bethlehem during the reign of Herod the Great. When the wise men came asking "Where is he that is born King of the Jews" Herod tried to eliminate Jesus by having all the male infants of the Bethlehem region put to death (Matt. 2:13-16). Mary and Joseph were warned by God in a dream to take the child and flee to Egypt where they stayed until Herod died.

Pontius Pilate the Roman procurator of Judea from A.D. 26-36 issued the order sentencing Jesus to death by crucifixion (Matt. 27; Mark 15; Luke 23; John 18-19) Unlike Herod, Pilate made little effort to be popular with the Jews of Judea. He angered the Jews when he took funds from the Temple treasury to build an aqueduct to supply water to Jerusalem. (*Nelson's Illustrated Bible Dictionary*, p. 842.) However Pilate gave into the Jewish leader's demands to sentence Jesus to death.

It may seem self evident why Satan wanted Jesus put to death and moved these two rulers to try and finally succeed in killing Him. But what was Satan's motivation? Was it just hatred of Jesus? What did Satan hope to accomplish by killing the Christ? The search for answers to these questions begins at the beginning of creation. After Adam's fall God had a very important conversation with Satan and Eve. God said: *"And I will put enmity between thee and the woman, and between thy seed and her seed; it shall bruise thy head, and thou shalt bruise his heel"*. (Genesis 3:15)

This is one of the most important verses in the bible. Charles H. Spurgeon said of this verse, "There lay within it, as an oak lies within an acorn, all the great truths which make up the gospel of Christ." (Sermon titled:, *Christ the Conqueror of Satan*, 1876) In fact among both Christians and Jews, many commentators consider Genesis 3:15 to be the first reference to a promised Messiah. For this reason it has been called the *protoevangelium*, or "first Gospel." it is the first promise of a Redeemer. Scofield calls it the "highway of the Seed." This fulfillment of God's promise of a seed (a single person) who will bruise (crush in the NIV) Satan's head runs from Abel, Seth, Noah (Gen. 6:8-10), Shem (Gen. 9:26-27), Abraham (Gen. 12:1-4), Isaac (Gen. 17:19-21), Jacob (Gen. 28:10-14), Judah (Gen. 49:10), David (2Sam. 7:5-17), Immanuel the Christ (Isa. 7:10-14; Matt. 1:1,20-23; John 12:31-33; 1 John 3:8). (Scofield, *The New Scofield Study Bible NAS* pages 8, 9)

On a side note have you ever wondered why Hebrew women considered it a curse not to be able have children? Nelson's Illustrated Bible Dictionary says of Michal the wife of David who criticized his dance at the return of the Ark of the Covenant: "Michael died barren (2 Sam. 6:21-23)—one of the most terrible fates that could befall a Hebrew woman." Some scholars think the answer is in this promised seed in Genesis 3:15. From Eve to Mary, Hebrew women hoped that they would be the mother to give birth to the promised Messiah. Indeed Eve said of her first born son Cain: " . . . *I have gotten a man from the LORD*." (Gen 4:1) Various translations and interpretations of this verse indicate that Eve may have believed that in bearing a son she was the highly favored mother of the Messiah. Thus it was that the bible says of Mary: *"highly favoured, the Lord is with thee: blessed art thou among women*." (Luke 1:28, 42)

Getting back to Genesis 3:15. In the King James Version the verse uses the word bruise to describe both what the devil does to the seed (Jesus) and what Jesus does to the devil. The NIV and other modern translations say the devil will *strike* His heel but Jesus will *crush* Satan's head. Satan struck the heel of Christ at Calvary but Jesus will crush Satan's head at the Great White Throne Judgment when he will cast Satan into the hell prepared for him and his angels (Matt. 25:41)

This Genesis prophecy also called the "crimson thread" unifies the entire bible. The entire bible both Old Testament and New Testament is about Jesus. As Jesus said:

- *"And beginning at Moses and all the prophets, he expounded unto them in all the scriptures the things concerning himself."* (Luke 24:27)
- *"Search the scriptures; for in them ye think ye have eternal life: and they are they which testify of me."* (John 5:39)
- *"And he said unto them, These are the words which I spake unto you, while I was yet with you, that all things must be fulfilled, which were written in the law of Moses, and in the prophets, and in the psalms, concerning me."* (Luke 24:44)
- *"Philip findeth Nathanael, and saith unto him, We have found him, of whom Moses in the law, and the prophets, did write, Jesus of Nazareth, the son of Joseph."* (John 1:45)
- *"Do not think that I will accuse you to the Father: there is one that accuseth you, even Moses, in whom ye trust. For had ye believed Moses, ye would have believed me: for he wrote of me."* (John 5:45-46)

To just sum up all these scriptures the bible says: "*Then said I, Lo, I come: in the volume of the book it is written of me,*" (Ps 40:7; Heb 10:7) So from Genesis 3:15 to the end of Revelation the entire bible is the working out and fulfilling of this prophetic statement as personified in the redeeming work of Christ. And no two characters are more central to this divine work than Herod the Great and Pontius Pilate.

From Herod to Pilate, Satan tried to identify and kill the one who will crush his head and send him to the everlasting fire prepared for him and his angels. (Matt 25:41) Satan could never be sure which woman might bring forth this person who would destroy him. Satan not only did not recognize Jesus as the one until it was too, late he also failed to realize that by moving Pilate to crucify Christ he was fulfilling the prophecy of Genesis 3:15. The crucifixion did not destroy Christ it only bruised His heel. "*But we speak the wisdom of God in a mystery, even the hidden wisdom, which God ordained before the world unto our glory: Which none of the princes of this world knew: for had they known it, they would not have crucified the Lord of glory.*" (1 Cor. 2:7-8, see also: Luke 23:34; Acts 3:17; John 16:3) The crucifixion of Christ sealed Satan's destiny. The heel of the seed had then been bruised but at the resurrection Satan realized that all that remained was for him to be crushed, destroyed and sent to everlasting torment in hell.

That period of time from Herod to Pilate when Jesus was born, lived and died for our sins is the most important 33 years in human history. Of these two men, I feel the greater sadness for Pilate. Herod never saw Jesus. He had very little knowledge of the role he was playing as a tool of Satan. But Pilate met and talked with Jesus. One of the saddest truths of human history is that Pilate looked upon Jesus and refused to love Him.

GOD WATCH BETWEEN ME & THEE

How many times have we heard this 'benediction': "*The LORD watch between me and thee, when we are absent one from another?*" These words are taken from Genesis 31:48. What a nice thing to say—right? Well perhaps not. A benediction is a *bene* or good diction or saying. It is where the speaker speaks a good word or blessing on the recipient. Is that what's going on here? Let's go to the source.

> *"Clearly suspicion permeated the entire arrangement."*

Gen 31:48-55

48 *And Laban said, This heap is a witness between me and thee this day. Therefore was the name of it called Galeed;*

49 *And Mizpah; for he said, The LORD watch between me and thee, when we are absent one from another.*

50 *If thou shalt afflict my daughters, or if thou shalt take other wives beside my daughters, no man is with us; see, God is witness betwixt me and thee.*

51 *And Laban said to Jacob, Behold this heap, and behold this pillar, which I have cast betwixt me and thee;*

52 *This heap be witness, and this pillar be witness, that I will not pass over this heap to thee, and that thou shalt not pass over this heap and this pillar unto me, for harm.*

53 *The God of Abraham, and the God of Nahor, the God of their father, judge betwixt us. And Jacob sware by the fear of his father Isaac.*

54 *Then Jacob offered sacrifice upon the mount, and called his brethren to eat bread: and they did eat bread, and tarried all night in the mount.*

55 *And early in the morning Laban rose up, and kissed his sons and his daughters, and blessed them: and Laban departed, and returned unto his place.*

Laban is not pronouncing a benediction on Jacob. Laban is saying that you have made promises by virtue of marrying my daughter. There is peace between us. But God is watching you when you are out of my sight, to insure that you keep your word. To insure that you treat my daughter well and do not break the nonaggression pact we have made here signified by the pillar and cairn (heap) as boundary markers.

Clearly suspicion permeated the entire arrangement and Laban was trying to assure Jacob's compliance by warning him that God would witness any transgression of their agreements and punish Jacob. Not exactly a 'good saying.' This verse when paraphrased in our current benediction has taken on a positive meaning quite at odds with its origin. Now the person pronouncing the benediction means that God exercising His good providence will watch over and bless the congregation as we leave each others presence in church. That's all right. Indeed see 1 Sam. 20:42 for similar words spoken by Jonathan to David. Words and phrases often grow and change with changes in popular usage. Just look at the word "gay." (James 2:3) But as ministers and preachers we have to be careful to be aware of the context and origin of scriptures that we quote or paraphrase so that our *dictions* will indeed be *bene*.

GOD'S STRANGE WORKS

God works in mysterious ways His wonders to perform. We have all heard that saying. I haven't found that saying in the bible but I have to admit that mysterious is sometimes the only way to describe how God works things out in my life and I am sure yours also. In fact I would go so far as to call God's actions strange at times. Yes I am calling God's actions at times strange. I hope no one takes offense at this apparently irreverent description of God's works because I have authority and permission to do so. Isaiah said: *"For the LORD shall rise up as in mount Perazim, he shall be wroth as in the valley of Gibeon, that he may do his work, his strange work; and bring to pass his act, his strange act"* (Isa. 28:21).

God realizes that from our perspective and even perhaps from His He works in ways that appear strange. But there is always a plan and purpose behind the working out of God's purposes for our lives. Looking back I can see how God was working things out to His glory and my good (Rom 8:28) in ways I could not have imagined.

Look at all that Joseph went through as God worked out His plan to save Egypt and Jacob's family from starvation. All this was just a part of God's outworking of His plan concerning the nation of Israel. We must also remember that as God works on His plan for our lives He is also working on the plans for the lives of those we come in contact with.

And look at God's greatest plan—the plan of salvation. God's predetermined plan to reconcile man to Himself. This plan was worked out in the counsels of heaven before the world was even created and we are living participants in this ultimately complex plan. (supra-lapsarianism).

So marvel not for the bible says of God: *"Who is like unto thee, O LORD, among the gods? who is like thee, glorious in holiness, fearful in praises, DOING WONDERS?"* (Exodus 15:11)

PAUL WARNED NOT
TO GO TO JERUSALEM

I now enter dangerous waters. The question this chapter addresses is whether Paul ventured out of the will of God in going to Jerusalem. I believe he was out of the will of God in going to Jerusalem. What saith the scriptures?

One thing is clear God the Holy Spirit on three occasions warned Paul not to go to Jerusalem. Note that after the first warning Paul says he did not know *"the things that shall befall me there (Jerusalem)."* After a second warning (Acts 21:4) the Holy Spirit makes it clear via the prophet, named Agabus what indeed was going to happen to Paul.

> **"But when it came to Jerusalem Paul did not heed the warnings or follow the Holy Spirit's instructions."**

So it is clear that the Holy Spirit warned Paul not to go to Jerusalem.

Acts 20:22-24

22 *And now, behold, I go bound in the spirit unto Jerusalem, not knowing the things that shall befall me there:*

23 *Save that the HOLY GHOST witnesseth in every city, saying that bonds and afflictions abide me.*

24 *But none of these things move me, neither count I my life dear unto myself, so that I might finish my course with joy, and the ministry, which I have received of the Lord Jesus, to testify the gospel of the grace of God.*

Some scholars like Charles C. Ryrie say that the words "bound in the spirit" mean that Paul was compelled by the Holy Spirit to go to Jerusalem. And the warnings were to let him know what was waiting for him there. Scofield however notes that the "s" in this word "spirit" is in the lower case ("s") not a capital "S" thus indicating not the Holy Spirit but Paul's own spirit or his own will compelled him to go to Jerusalem.

Also note *the verse below:* "that he should not go up to Jerusalem." And Acts 21:10-15 where the Holy Ghost by the prophet Agabus "bessought him not to go up to Jerusalem."

This language is clear that the Holy Spirit was not only warning Paul of the danger and persecution he would face in Jerusalem but warning him NOT TO GO TO JERUSALEM.

Acts 21:4

4 And finding disciples, we tarried there seven days: who said to Paul through the *Spirit, that he should not go up to Jerusalem.*

Acts 21:10-15

10 *And as we tarried there many days, there came down from Judaea a certain prophet, named Agabus.*

11 *And when he was come unto us, he took Paul's girdle, and bound his own hands and feet, and said, Thus saith the HOLY GHOST, So shall the Jews at Jerusalem bind the man that owneth this girdle, and shall deliver him into the hands of the Gentiles.*

12 *And when we heard these things, both we, and they of that place,* **besought him not to go up to Jerusalem.**

13 *Then Paul answered, What mean ye to weep and to break mine heart? for I am ready not to be bound only, but also to die at Jerusalem for the name of the Lord Jesus.*

14 *And when he would not be persuaded, we ceased, saying, The will of the Lord be done.*

15 *And after those days we took up our carriages, and went up to Jerusalem.*

Recall another time the Holy Spirit intervened in Paul's travels:

Acts 16:6-10

6 *Now when they had gone throughout Phrygia and the region of Galatia, and were forbidden of the Holy Ghost to preach the word in Asia,*

7 *After they were come to Mysia, they assayed to go into Bithynia: but the Spirit suffered them not.*

8 *And they passing by Mysia came down to Troas.*

9 *And a vision appeared to Paul in the night; There stood a man of Macedonia, and prayed him, saying, Come over into Macedonia, and help us.*

> 10 *And after he had seen the vision, immediately we endeavoured to go into Macedonia, assuredly gathering that the Lord had called us for to preach the gospel unto them.*

So here there is no speculation about whether the Holy Spirit really meant what He said. Paul obeyed the Holy Spirit and the vision and did not preach in Asia but traveled to Macedonia. But when it came to Jerusalem Paul did not heed the warnings or follow the Holy Spirit's instructions. Why? I think these verses shed some light on the question:

Rom 10:1
> 1 *Brethren, my heart's desire and prayer to God for Israel is, that they might be saved.*

Paul loved his Jewish brethren. He was not only willing to die in his zeal to see Israel saved he was willing if it were possible to forfeit his own salvation if possible for their sakes. *"That I have great heaviness and continual sorrow in my heart. For I could wish that myself were accursed from Christ for my brethren, my kinsmen according to the flesh."* (Rom 9:2-3)

"Brethren, my heart's desire and prayer to God for Israel is, that they might be saved." (Rom 10:1)

Paul was no stranger to persecution. There was a plot against Paul's life in Damascus. In Lystra he was stoned and left for dead (Acts 14:19). He was imprisoned in Philippi (Acts 16:19-24). He was forced to flee Thessalonica (Acts 17:5-10) he was persecuted by the Hellenists in Jerusalem (Acts 9:29). He was constantly harassed by Jews (Acts 13:50); 14:2, 5, 19; 16:19-24; 17:5-9). He was even assaulted by the worshipers of Artemis (Acts 19:21-41).

Paul's missionary life was in constant danger and legal difficulties. He himself complains of the beatings and vilifications that he withstood (2 Cor. 11:22-29; I Cor. 4:9). Indeed wherever Paul's mission took him, trouble and persecution followed. And in fact Paul rejoiced that he *"was counted worthy to suffer shame for his name."* (Acts 5:41).

But the difference with Jerusalem was that here the Holy Spirit specifically warned Paul of the danger and told him not to go, but he did and set in motion events that lead to the end of his life.

REAL POWER

I was lying on the floor in the gym of Tougaloo College about three in the morning June 25, 1966 thinking about power—Black Power. On June 6 James Meredith the first black student to attend the University of Mississippi in 1962 was wounded by three shotgun blast to his head, shoulder, back and legs. This happened while he walked from Memphis, Tennessee to Jackson, Mississippi to encourage African Americans to register and vote. He called it a "march against fear."

The next day, leaders of the major civil rights organizations, Dr. Martin Luther King of the SCLC (Southern Christian Leadership Conference), Floyd McKissick of CORE (Congress of Racial Equality) and Stokely Carmichael (Kwame Ture) of SNCC (Student Non-Violent Co-coordinating Committee), announced that they would complete his march, and invited freedom-loving people from all over the country to join them.

"Their hearts were not changed but their bank accounts were."

For almost three weeks, between a few hundred and a several thousand people walked the 220 miles to the Mississippi state capitol, camping out at night under rented circus tents and in this gym. Local people fed the marchers on the way. After asking that federal registrars be sent to Mississippi, civil rights leaders took groups of marchers to nearby towns to canvass, rally and register local African Americans. The Department of Justice later estimated that between 2,500 and 3,000 black Mississippians were registered to vote during the march.

When the marchers got to Greenwood, Mississippi, Stokely Carmichael and some of the other marchers were arrested by the police. It was the 27th time that Carmichael had been arrested and on his release on the 16th of June, he made his famous *Black Power* speech. Carmichael called for "black people in this country to unite, to recognize their heritage, and to build a sense of community". He also advocated that African Americans should form and lead their own organizations and reject the values of American society.

I was on that march and that night at Tougaloo College was the last night of the march. The next morning we would walk the last ten miles to Jackson. I could not sleep thinking about all that had happened and what would happen tomorrow. But the idea that was most responsible for keeping me awake was the phrase "Black Power." We did not know exactly what it meant but it sure sounded good. Black Power!

As the years went by and the Civil Rights movement progressed there were victories with Civil Rights legislation and defeats with the death of Dr. King I became cynical about one of the primary assumptions of the movement. That being the purpose of non-violent activism was to "prick the conscience of the nation." I came to the conclusion the nation had no conscience to prick.

So what should my response be? I noticed that when southern juries acquitted numerous white persons accused of attacking civil rights workers that the United States government would file Civil Rights complaints against these men. The thing that interested me about these suits was not the substance or the merits of the litigation. What I found interesting was the time and expense the defendants were put to in defending themselves. For example those police officers who beat Rodney King I'm sure had little or no moral regrets about what they did. But by the time all the litigation was finished they had been put to enormous expense defending themselves. I have no doubt they wished they had not laid a hand or night stick on Mr. King. Their hearts were not changed but their bank accounts were.

It was that realization that the law provided an individual with the power to take meaningful action against evil that motivated me to go to law school. That kind of power is emotionally satisfying but incomplete. There is a power that comes into our lives when we receive Christ that is beyond any earthly experience. The power of the indwelling of the Holy Spirit. *"And, behold, I send the promise of my Father upon you: but tarry ye in the city of Jerusalem, until ye be endued with power from on high."* (Luke 24:49) Our desire for personal power is an outgrowth of the goals we have in life. We want power to affect our job security. We want power to influence our children, spouses and people who we love and/or can affect our lives for good or bad. We do not like the feeling of being helpless or powerless.

But we as Christians have total power in our total surrender to Christ. God has a plan for our lives and God is *"able to keep that which I have committed unto him against that day."* (2 Tim 1:12) So much of the stress we suffer day by day is a result of not being able to rely on the promises of God. For nine years I worked for the Chicago Housing Authority. It was the most stressful nine years of my life. The main source of the stress was that there were always people plotting to cause me trouble. So I was constantly acting and reacting to these attacks. Looking back I realize that it was God's plan that I had that job long enough to pay my school loans, pay off our mortgage and other expenses before calling me into the ministry. Therefore I could have rested in the assurance that God was in control. "Oh what peace we often forfeit. Oh what needless pain we bear all because we do not carry everything to God in prayer."

Every problem we face, God is the answer. Every challenge that confronts us, God is the answer. And God shares his strategies and comforts with us through His word and the still quite voice of the Holy Spirit. Look at the apostles. Most of these men fled in fear when Jesus was arrested. Yet after the Holy Spirit had come upon them it was said of them: "*These that have turned the world upside down are come hither also.*" (Acts 17:6) Power is not just having ability and influence but knowing you have it.

Think of the power God entrust to us ministers. He trusts us to take the Gospel to his people. The Gospel is not just words "*it is the power of God unto salvation to every one that believeth . . .*" (Rom 1:16) Think about it, God has entrusted us with the message that calls people "*out of darkness into his marvelous light.*" (1 Peter 2:9) As we see people on the street, on our jobs or in other places we have the words of life. As the song says: "Beautiful words; wonderful words; wonderful words of life." Now that's real power!

SINNERS GOD "HATES"

We have all heard the saying: "God hates sin but loves the sinner." After all doesn't the bible say that God so loved the world . . . ? So we have a cozy warm feeling about God looking down on sinners of all kinds with a benign tolerant love for any and all sinners no matter what.

> "God has a particular dislike for people that cause dissension in the church."

Well my fellow Bereans (Acts 17:10, 11) let us search the scriptures to see "*whether those things (are) so.*" The bible says: "*The foolish shall not stand in thy sight: thou hatest all workers of iniquity.*" (Ps 5:5-6) and "*The LORD trieth the righteous; but the wicked and him that loveth violence his soul hateth.*" (Psalms 11:5) and:

Prov. 6:16-19

*16 These six things doth the LORD **hate**: yea, seven are an abomination unto him:*

17 A proud look, a lying tongue, and hands that shed innocent blood,

18 An heart that deviseth wicked imaginations, feet that be swift in running to mischief,

19 A false witness that speaketh lies, and he that soweth discord among brethren.

Of all these scriptures this passage in Proverbs seems to be the clearest scripture for the proposition that there is a certain category of sinner that the bible says God hates, namely: people who cause discord among brethren and people that cause division and strife in the church. Note what Paul says: "*Now I beseech you, brethren, mark them which cause divisions and offences contrary to the doctrine which ye have learned; and avoid them. For they that are such serve not our Lord Jesus Christ, but their own belly; and by good words and fair speeches deceive the hearts of the simple.*" (Romans 16:17, 18).

God has a particular dislike for people that cause dissension in the church. After all the command that we Christians love one another is one of the most often repeated directions in the bible: *"A new commandment I give unto you, That ye love one another; as I have loved you, that ye also love one another."* (Jn. 13:34) see also: (Jn. 15:12; Jn. 15:17; Rom. 13:8; Rom. 13:8; 1Thes. 4:9; 1 Pet. 1:22; I Jn. 3:11; I Jn. 3:23; I Jn. 4:7; I Jn. 4:11 and I Jn. 4:12) just to cite a few.

So what have we learned? God is particularly interested in his children loving one another. In fact it is so important that it is an indicator that one is in fact a Christian. *We know that we have passed from death unto life, because we love the brethren. He that loveth not his brother abideth in death."* (I Jn 3:14 see also John 13:35) Strong language but it is the Word of God. This may indicate why the bible says God hates anyone that soweth discord among brethren.

STRANGE FIRE—
NEW AGE CHRISTIANITY

Bishop Arthur Brazier Pastor of the Apostolic Church of God in Chicago once mentioned reports of African American ministers mixing Christian worship with beliefs and practices of Sun Myung Moon. It is amazing to think that ministers of the Gospel believe that they can decide to alter the

> **"God was saying to Cain; just worship me in the way I require and all will be well. But Cain was stubborn."**

requirement that we worship God only and only in the manner He prescribes. It is a serious matter to follow our own feelings in matters concerning the lordship and worship of God.

Jesus said: *"Jesus saith unto him, I am the way, the truth, and the life: no man cometh unto the Father, but by me."* (John 14:6) God the Father says: *"I, even I, am the LORD; and beside me there is no saviour."* (Isa. 43:12) There are 160 verses in the bible where God states: 'I am the Lord'. (From Gen. 15:7 to Mal. 3:6) We can conclude that God takes His Lordship seriously—and so should we. To most of us this truth seems obvious. But some Christians have begun to worship in ways that are inconsistent with the exclusive claims of God. God does not tolerate indifferent or improper worship in the scriptures. The bible describes several examples of people who approached God in their own way and suffered judgment, discipline and death as a result. (*Deception*, Ministry Today Nov/Dec 2006 p. 46)

In Gen. 4 we read of God's reaction to the sacrifice of Cain: *"And in process of time it came to pass, that Cain brought of the fruit of the ground an offering unto the LORD. And Abel, he also brought of the firstlings of his flock and of the fat thereof. And the LORD had respect unto Abel and to his offering: But unto Cain and to his offering he had not respect. And Cain was very wroth, and his countenance fell. And the LORD said unto Cain, Why art thou wroth? and why is thy countenance fallen? If thou doest well, shalt thou not be accepted? and if thou doest not well, sin lieth at the door . . . ."* (Gen 4:3-7) God was saying to Cain; just worship me in the way I require and all will be well. But Cain was stubborn. He seems reasonable that it should not matter what offering he brings as long as he was sincere. God should accept my sincere offering even if it is not exactly what God demands. What's the difference? 'God knows my heart.' It was not for Cain to reason why God required an animal offering it was for Cain to obey.

Consider 1Sam. 15, where Samuel upbraids Saul for disobedience: *"And the LORD sent thee on a journey, and said, Go and utterly destroy the sinners the Amalekites, and fight against them until they be consumed. Wherefore then didst thou not obey the voice of the LORD, but didst fly upon the spoil, and didst evil in the sight of the LORD? And Saul said unto Samuel, Yea, I have obeyed the voice of the LORD . . . But the people took of the spoil, sheep and oxen, the chief of the things which should have been utterly destroyed, to sacrifice unto the LORD thy God . . . And Samuel said, Hath the LORD as great delight in burnt offerings and sacrifices, as in obeying the voice of the LORD? Behold, to obey is better than sacrifice, and to hearken than the fat of rams."* (1 Sam. 15:18-22) Here even though the sacrifice was correct in form the offering was improperly obtained. And it cost Saul his crown.

In 1Chron. 13:7-12 we read the sad story of Uzza who improperly transported and touched the ark of God. (Ex 37:5, Deut 10:8 etc) And his error cost Uzza his life: *"And when they came unto the threshingfloor of Chidon, Uzza who put forth his hand to hold the ark; for the oxen stumbled. And the anger of the LORD was kindled against Uzza, and he smote him, because he put his hand to the ark: and there he died before God."* (1 Chron. 13:9,10)

In Leviticus 10 we read of Nadab and Abihu's strange fire. *"And Nadab and Abihu, the sons of Aaron, took either of them his censer, and put fire therein, and put incense thereon, and offered strange fire before the LORD, which he commanded them not. And there went out fire from the LORD, and devoured them, and they died before the LORD."* (Verses 1, 2 See Ex. 30:9) It appears they may have used coals of fire that were not taken from the brazen altar as prescribed (see Lev. 6:12-13; 16:12). They may also have offered incense other than at the morning or evening sacrifice (cf. Ex. 30:7-8). They may have been drunk because a prohibition against drinking immediately follows their punishment (v. 9). In any event they failed to worship God in the manner God required and it cost them their lives. (*Ryrie Study Bible Expanded Edition* note on Lev. 10:1).

Paul reports that impetuous taking of communion cost "many" worshipers their lives: "*For he that eateth and drinketh unworthily, eateth and drinketh damnation to himself, not discerning the Lord's body. For this cause many are weak and sickly among you, and many sleep.*" (1 Cor. 11:29-30)

We live in a time when Christians are mixing New Age practices with the worship of God Almighty. (See: *Running Against the Wind*, Brian Flynn founder of One Truth Ministries (*www.onetruthministries.com*). Some churches allow a practice called *lectio divina* that some believe uses scriptures as a mantra in meditation. Some Christians practice a form of what they call "Christian Yoga, also known as "Chroga" which incorporates meditations on Christ into yoga postures. These so called churches are sometimes called Christian yoga ministries.

The idea of new age meditations and yoga being mixed with Christian worship is controversial. The advocates say stretching and meditating are harmless practices. But Brian Flynn of One Truth Ministries notes, "Meditations are not the only problem. It is a whole series of ritual appreciations to the sun, (and) being thankful for the source of energy." (*Deception*, Ministry Today p.46) Jesus said: "*But the hour cometh, and now is, when the true worshippers shall worship the Father in spirit and in truth: for the Father seeketh such to worship him. God is a Spirit: and they that worship him must worship him in spirit and in truth.*" (John 4:23-24) Note Jesus said spirit AND truth. Spiritual worship is commanded but it must be ordered by truth. As the examples given at the beginning of this article show God is serious about how we are to approach Him in worship. Churches mixing unusual practices with worship may be sincere but God says: "*to obey is better than sacrifice, and to hearken than the fat of rams.*" (1 Sam. 15:22)

These developments should not come as a surprise to bible students. Jesus said of the times just before His return: "*That ye be not soon shaken in mind, or be troubled, neither by spirit, nor by word, nor by letter as from us, as that the day of Christ is at hand. Let no man deceive you by any means: for that day shall not come, except there come a falling away first, and that man of sin be revealed, the son of perdition;*" (2 Thess. 2:2-3) This apostasy will occur in the church. As Paul wrote to Timothy: "*For the time will come when they will not endure sound doctrine; but after their own lusts shall they heap to themselves teachers, having itching ears; And they shall turn away their ears from the truth, and shall be turned unto fables.*" (2 Tim 4:3-4) I believe the mixing of new age philosophy with Christianity is a sure sign "*that the day of Christ is at hand.*"

Indeed we have recently seen a prominent African American minister joining the Nation of Islam led by Minister Louis Farakhan. And yea another African American protestant Bishop who now believes that all people will go to heaven and no one will go to hell because he does not believe there is such a place. This despite the clear teaching of Jesus. (Matt. 24:41)

We ministers must be vigilant to oppose any doctrine or practice that weakens the Gospel message. The true church cannot be salt and light if it is mixed with the leaven of the world. Our feelings, thoughts and experiences are not the standards. The Word of God is the rule and standard by which we approach the throne of God. And we know how God values His Word, as David said: *"for thou hast magnified thy word above all thy name."* (Ps 138:2) The church must take care lest we offer strange fire to God and be consumed thereby.

THE SUFFERING OF CHRIST

Jesus suffered hours of physical pain before and during His crucifixion. He was scourged He was spit upon, nails were driven through his hands and feet and a spear pierced his side (Matt. 20:19; Mark 10:34; John 19:34). His physical suffering was so great that people who saw him were astonished that His "visage was so marred more than any man and his form more than the sons of men :"(Isa. 52:14).

I want to focus now on an area of our Lord's suffering not often discussed or described. It is not described because it can't be described in words. That is the suffering of Jesus when God the Father made Jesus to become sin for us. "He made him who knew no sin to be sin for us" (2Corinthians 5:21). Think about it! " . . . the LORD hath laid on him the iniquity of us all" (Isaiah 53:6).

My point is that as great as Christ' physical suffering at the hands of men, I believe it did not compare with what God the Father poured out on Him in punishing Jesus for all of the sins of mankind. As Bishop Brazier once said: "God put Jesus on the cross." Sure the Jews accused Him and the Romans abused Him but it was the Father that put Jesus on that cross and poured out wrath upon him that should have been poured out on us. "Yet it pleased the Lord to bruise him" (Isaiah 53:10). "He spared not his own Son, but delivered him up for us all . . ." (Romans 8:32; see also John 3:16).

I do not diminish the physical suffering of Christ. For it was the shed blood of Christ that redeemed us. But I want to add to our appreciation of what the Romans did to Christ an appreciation of what He suffered under the punishing hand of the Father. And perhaps worst of all God turned his back on Jesus causing Jesus to cry with a loud voice, "*Eli, Eli, lama sabachthani*? that is to say, My God, my God, why hast thou forsaken me?" (Matt 27:46). And because Jesus was "forsaken" God says to us: "I will never leave thee nor forsake thee" (Hebrews 13:5). We must praise and thank God for the suffering Jesus endured that words cannot describe.

TITHING IN THE NEW TESTAMENT

The purpose of this chapter is not to make the case for tithing. Many Christians know what the scriptures say concerning tithing. Tithing was before the Law of Moses (Gen 14:18-20) and under the Law (Lev 27:30 etc).

> *Gen 14:18-20*
> *18 And Melchizedek king of Salem brought forth bread and wine: and he was the priest of the most high God.*
> *19 And he blessed him, and said, Blessed be Abram of the most high God, possessor of heaven and earth:*
> *20 And blessed be the most high God, which hath delivered thine enemies into thy hand. And he gave him tithes of all.*

> *Lev 27:30*
> *30 And all the tithe of the land, whether of the seed of the land, or of the fruit of the tree, is the LORD's: it is holy unto the LORD.*

There is however, discussion concerning whether tithing is prescribed in the New Testament. All of us who tithe do not need to be convinced that tithing is for today and that the blessings promised in the scriptures (Mal 3:10) to those who tithe inure to our benefit when we give God the sacred tenth of our increase.

> *Mal 3:10*
> *10 Bring ye all the tithes into the storehouse, that there may be meat in mine house, and prove me now herewith, saith the LORD of hosts, if I will not open you the windows of heaven, and pour you out a blessing, that there shall not be room enough to receive it. (KJV)*

However I would like to suggest a scripture for consideration when we are pressed on the question of whether tithing is prescribed in the New Testament. Consider Matt 23:23.

> *Matt 23:23*
> 23 *Woe unto you, scribes and Pharisees, hypocrites! for ye pay tithe*
>   *of mint and anise and cummin, and have omitted the weightier*
>   *matters of the law, judgment, mercy, and faith: these ought ye to*
>   *have done, and not to leave the other undone.*
>   *(KJV)*

The verse is somewhat clearer in the modern translations.

> *Matt 23:23*
> 23 *"Woe to you, teachers of the law and Pharisees, you hypocrites!*
>   *You give a tenth of your spices—mint, dill and cummin. But you*
>   *have neglected the more important matters of the law—justice,*
>   *mercy and faithfulness. You should have practiced the latter,*
>   *without neglecting the former.*
>   *(NIV)*

> *Matt 23:23*
>
> 23 *How terrible it will be for you teachers of religious law and*
>   *you Pharisees. Hypocrites! For you are careful to tithe even the*
>   *tiniest part of your income, but you ignore the important things*
>   *of the law—justice, mercy, and faith. You should tithe, yes, but*
>   *you should not leave undone the more important things.*
>   *(NLT)*

In this verse Jesus is castigating the Pharisees for not practicing "judgment, mercy, and faith" (KJV) or as the NIV states "justice, mercy and faithfulness." In making this statement Jesus notes with approval that they do "pay tithe" (KJV) or " . . . give a tenth" (NIV). Then after noting that they tithe Jesus says in the New Living Translation, "you should tithe . . ." In the NIV Jesus says you should not neglect the "former" that being giving the "tenth." In all three translations our Lord and savior Jesus Christ tells these people they should tithe.

Admittedly tithing is not the main point of this scripture. Jesus makes the point that tithing did not replace the obligation to do justice, mercy and faithfulness, which was His main point. So the lesson of the scripture is that in addition to tithing people should attend to the weightier or more important matters of justice, mercy and faithfulness. We of course agree that tithing in the absence of compassion, justice, mercy and faithfulness would not be pleasing to God. But in making this point our Lord clearly states that tithing is something that also ought to be done. And this statement is in the New Testament.

So the next time someone makes the statement that tithing is an Old Testament doctrine refer him or her to Matt. 23:23. Read it carefully and be prepared to discuss it in context but it is another argument in favor of our continued giving of the sacred tenth back to God.

WHO'S DOING THE TALKING?

"Thou shalt also decree a thing, and it shall be established unto thee: and the light shall shine upon thy ways." (Job 22:28) This verse is a great encouragement in times of need. It is not my intention to discourage the use of this scripture as a blessing to the body of Christ. However, let's take a closer look at this verse.

It is a basic principle of hermeneutics that we have to understand the context of scriptures to understand the content of scriptures. One factor in understanding the context of a verse is to ask: "Who is doing the talking?" Is it someone we can trust like Daniel, Abraham or God? Is it someone whose words may not be trustworthy like Satan?

Who is talking in this verse? In the book of Job many chapters begin by telling us who will be the primary speaker in the chapter. Job 22:1 reads: *"Then Eliphaz the Temanite answered and said,"* The remainder of chapter 22 is Eliphaz telling Job that if he would repent and return to God all would be well with Job (see Job 22:23). Well let's look at what God has to say.

Job 42:7-8
7   *And it was so, that after the LORD had spoken these words unto Job, the LORD said to Eliphaz the Temanite, My wrath is kindled against thee, and against thy two friends: for ye have not spoken of me the thing that is right, as my servant Job hath.*
8   *Therefore take unto you now seven bullocks and seven rams, and go to my servant Job, and offer up for yourselves a burnt offering; and my servant Job shall pray for you: for him will I accept: lest I deal with you after your folly, in that ye have not spoken of me the thing which is right, like my servant Job.*

What was that God said about Eliphaz? " . . . in that ye have not spoken of me the thing which is right, like my servant Job." God said Eliphaz did not know what he was talking about. So we must be very careful quoting and relying on the any words spoken by Eliphaz, Bildad, Zophar and Elihu. These "friends" of Job stated many laudable principles in their criticism of Job. But the principles did not apply to Job. Job had not sinned (Job 1:1). Job was not being punished by God. So the scripture in verse 28 standing alone is a wonderful verse but in context we have to be careful. When using this verse perhaps some comment should be made to let the people know that we understand the context of this wonderful verse. For indeed when you decree a thing it shall be established unto thee: and the light shall shine upon thy ways. Praise The Lord!

WHO WILL BE MAYOR OF CHICAGO—DURING THE MILLENNIAL KINGDOM?

As we prepare to vote there are several candidates vying for the position of Mayor of Chicago. They are striving mightily and spending large sums of money to achieve the prize of being the one in charge of the city and other divisions of government. Consider that there will come a time when Jesus will assign rulers over the cities of the earth—including Chicago. And the faithful saints will reign and rule over the cities and nations with Christ. No election, no campaign a direct appointment by our Lord!

First some background. (For a detailed discussion of various views on eschatology see *Things To Come* by J. Dwight Pentecost.) The end times are indeed plural. That is there will not just be one last day for the world when Jesus takes the saints to heaven and consigns the lost to hell. The end times consist of several apocalyptic events culminating in the Eternal State where the saints live forever in the New Jerusalem with God. The next event on God's calendar is the catching away of the saints by Jesus in the air to be taken to heaven. This event is imminent in the sense that no preceding events have to occur prior to the Rapture. It could happen at any second. Maranatha.

After the Rapture comes the judgment of the saints at the Judgment Seat of Christ (*Bema*). This judgment takes place in heaven so it does not determine whether or not the Christian is going to heaven. We will already be there and that is wonderful but it is a serious judgment nonetheless. The Bible says of this judgment: "*For we must all appear before the judgment seat of Christ; that every one may receive the things done in his body, according to that he hath done, whether it be good or bad. Knowing therefore the terror of the Lord . . .*" (2 Cor. 5:10-11a) Paul says: ". . . *for we shall all stand before the judgment seat of Christ, so then every one of us shall give account of himself to God."* (Rom 14:10b-12) That "WE" and "US" refers to Christians.

There are serious negative consequences at this judgment. We are all familiar with the idea of receiving crowns and rewards at this judgment but the Bible says some Christians will "suffer loss!" *"Every man's work shall be made manifest: for the day shall declare it, because it shall be revealed by fire; and the fire shall try every man's work of what sort it is. If any man's work abide which he hath built thereupon, he shall receive a reward. If any man's work shall be burned, he shall suffer loss: but he himself shall be saved; yet so as by fire."* (1 Cor. 3:13-15) "SUFFER LOSS." This is loss of rewards but I believe beyond that there will be real suffering in the heart of the believer as Jesus reveals and judges the lives we have led since our salvation. Imagine the pain of looking into the face of Jesus who died for us and experiencing his judgment and disappointment at our failure to bear the fruit He intended us to produce.

How this loss will manifest itself is the subject of differing interpretations. Some scholars believe that some saints will not be permitted into the Marriage Supper of the Lamb (Rev 19:7-16) but will be consigned to the darkness outside the banquet hall (not the outer darkness of hell). (See: *The Reign of the Servant Kings* by Joseph C. Dillow) Others say no such casting out will occur (See: *The Glory of Heaven* by John F. Macarthur). Either way we should be vigilant to keep short accounts with God and fall on our face in confession when we miss the mark. And this is more important for ministers because we will be judged more severely than others. *"My brethren, be not many masters, knowing that we shall receive the greater condemnation."* (James 3:1)

This is the answer to the charge that eternal security means that a Christian can live 'any old way' and still go to heaven. The implication being that a Christian whose life is not exemplary gets away with sin because he or she is secure in salvation. No such thing. Jesus Himself will judge the behavior of all of us from the time of our salvation till we see him. Nobody gets away with anything.

Now to the good part. To those whose works survive this judgment as gold, silver and precious stones (1 Cor. 3:12) they will reign and rule with Christ. *"Blessed and holy is he that hath part in the first resurrection: on such the second death hath no power, but they shall be priests of God and of Christ, and shall reign with him a thousand years."* (Rev 20:6 see also 2 Tim 2:12) Jesus even speaks in a parable of rewarding the faithful servants with rulership over ten cities in the kingdom: *"and he said unto him, Well, thou good servant: because thou hast been faithful in a very little, have thou authority over ten cities."* (Luke 19:17)

Does this mean that some saints will literally rule over ten cities on the earth in the Millennial Kingdom? I do not know. Certainly those faithful servants will experience the joy of participating with Christ in His rulership over the kingdom. "We may not know exactly what our role will be, but we can assume it will be consistent with the uniqueness with which He created each of us, and it will be wonderful." (Dillow, pp 590) For sure when we return with Christ to the earth and He sets up His Kingdom (Isa. 9:6) there will be the cities on the earth as they are now. And someone will have authority over them. Christ will literally come to this earth, reside in Jerusalem and govern and the faithful will govern with Him. So someone will probably be in charge of Chicago (or whatever name Christ may give this city). Think of a possible thousand year term as mayor (or whatever the title will be) of Chicago. No primary or general election but a direct appointment by the King. It is worth it to preserve in holiness till the end—an end that is really just the beginning

DO IT NOW!

A few weeks ago I was in a hurry to get to court and I went through a stop sign I did not notice. As I was going through the intersection I saw another car to my right and for some reason I was sure that car had a stop sign and would surely stop. The driver of that car seeing I had the stop sign assumed I would stop. So we headed straight for each other. We both slammed on our brakes and the brakes did their job as we came within no more than two or three inches of colliding.

A little later as I was driving I remembered that when I left home and got into my car I prayed a short prayer asking God to give me journey mercies and I remember saying "and no accidents Lord in Jesus name." I believe that but for that prayer with the specific request for "no accidents" I would have caused a terrible accident that morning. It was my calling on the name of the Lord that made the difference.

> *"Therefore, since we have this precious privilege we should use it continually."*

We know there are times when we all call on the name of the Lord. When we pray for ourselves and others we are calling on His name. When we are under persecution or temptation we call upon His name for "*God is our refuge and strength, a very present help in trouble.*" (Ps 46:1) Sometimes when I visit the sick in hospitals especially in the ICUs where the rooms are often in a circle around the nurse's station, I look at the various rooms noticing the patients and their families. I wonder if the patients and families are saved. Do they know the Lord? Imagine you are in a hospital with a serious illness and you do not know Jesus. What do you do? Who do you call upon for healing and comfort? In what or who do you place your hope? To go through life without the wonderful privilege and comfort of calling on our savior is too awful to imagine.

Therefore, since we have this precious privilege we should use it continually. Remember when we were kids; we had a saying when someone would call out our name: "Yes that's my name, don't wear it out"? Well we cannot wear out the name of Jesus. If anything we don't use His name enough. Satan does not want us using the name of Jesus and when we miss the mark he will try to shame us into not calling on the name of the Lord. He will tell us that we are not worthy to pray and that God is tired of us confessing the same sins over and over. He tells us that God knows we have not really repented and we are going to do it again. Does any of this sound familiar or am I the only one? It's the time to cry out the loudest: Jesus! Jesus! Jesus!

Remember the publican, " . . . *standing afar off, would not lift up so much as his eyes unto heaven, but smote upon his breast, saying, God be merciful to me a sinner." Jesus said: "I tell you, this man went down to his house justified rather than the other: for every one that exalteth himself shall be abased; and he that humbleth himself shall be exalted."* (Luke 18:13-14) So one of the best times to call on the name of the Lord is when we least deserve to. Oh what peace we often forfeit—oh what needless pain we bear all because we do not carry everything to the Lord in prayer.

How about in times of doubt: a doubt that goes to the core of our beliefs? What if all we believe is not true? Have you ever thought that? Is there really a heaven? These kinds of thoughts are disturbing and most ministers don't have them, but some do. Satan the author of such doubts will try to make such a minister think he or she is not worthy to preach the gospel. What does the Bible say? We as ministers take personally Christ's great commission to His disciples. But look at the verses just preceding the commission: "*Then the eleven disciples went away into Galilee, into a mountain where Jesus had appointed them. And when they saw him, they worshipped him: but some doubted. And Jesus came and spake unto them, saying, All power is given unto me in heaven and in earth. Go ye therefore, and teach all nations, baptizing them in the name of the Father, and of the Son, and of the Holy Ghost: Teaching them to observe all things whatsoever I have commanded you: and, lo, I am with you alway, even unto the end of the world. Amen."* (Matt 28:16-20) Their doubts did not disqualify these men from ministry. Their faith was important not an occasional attack of doubt.

A soldier receives the Medal of Honor for acts of bravery in the face of fear not because he has no fear but because he overcame fear. Faith overcomes doubt. What then should be done with these thoughts?

Remember the man whose son had a dumb spirit; (Mark 9:17) "*Jesus said unto him, If thou canst believe, all things are possible to him that believeth. And straightway the father of the child cried out, and said with tears, Lord, I believe; help thou mine unbelief.*" (Mark 9:23-24)

Jesus required belief from the man and the man did believe up to a point. But the man knew that in his heart he had doubt about Jesus and His power to heal. But he took his doubt to Jesus. He called on the name of the Lord and Jesus responded. Faith in God is not a matter of logic. It is not a purely intellectual process. Faith is a gift. "*For by grace are ye saved through faith; and that not of yourselves: it is the gift of God :*"

(Eph 2:8) The very God that requires faith from us is the God who gives us the faith He requires!

Jesus will always hear us when we call upon his name. Always! Don't you respond when you hear your name called? So does our Lord. The Bible says: "*Then they that feared the LORD spake often one to another: and the LORD hearkened, and heard it, and a book of remembrance was written before him for them that feared the LORD, and that thought upon his name.*" (Mal 3:16) Note that this book of remembrance is written before God for just thinking upon His name; how much more will God respond to those who call on the name of our Lord and Savior Jesus Christ. There are no circumstances so dire, sinful or wrong that should stop us from calling on the name of the Lord. He is waiting for that call and He will answer. We should be continually calling on His precious name. The Bible says Pray without ceasing. (1 Thess 5:17 see also Acts 12:5)

So when should we call on the name of the Lord—RIGHT NOW!

THE POWER OF POSITIVE ACTION

One of the first books I read at the age of about eleven was *The Power of Positive Thinking* by Dr. Norman Vincent Peale. The theme of this book is that thinking positively often results in a positive outcome to situations and challenges. This is true. But what do you do if you tend to think negatively—like I do! I When confronted with a challenge I tend to expect things not to work out well. When I attempt some positive step in my life I expect difficulties and do not assume success.

For example when I got out of the Army the only job I could get with my high school diploma was working in a factory (The Dresser Mfg. Co.) on 13th and Kostner. After a year or so I had a strong urge to try to do better. I did not know what I could do with my life but I decided to try, I went to Kennedy-King Jr. College (KKC). I did not expect to finish I just wanted to go to school.

I got an Associate of Arts (AA) degree from KKC. Afterwards, some of the teachers there encouraged to me apply to the University of Chicago (U of C) as a transfer student. I applied not expecting to be admitted, through miraculous interventions by God (perhaps I will tell the whole story in another article), I was admitted and much to my surprise I received a Bachelor of Arts (BA) degree from U of C. One of my history professors there, John Hope Franklin, suggested I go to law school. So I applied to Northwestern not expecting to be admitted; I was. I started classes not believing I would actually finish and get a law degree; I did. I took the Bar exam not expecting to pass and I didn't: I took it again, passed and obtained a license to practice law.

What am I saying by recounting these experiences? I think a better title for Dr. Peale's book might be, The Power of Positive Action. I have been in many challenging situations such as in Vietnam as well other circumstances. And if you will permit me I will state Anderson's Rule for overcoming a difficult situation. "Positive action is more important than positive thinking." Positive action is often based on hope rather than faith. When a person takes a positive step in the face of overwhelming odds I don't think it is often based on believing things will work out so much as hoping they will.

> "Positive action is more important than positive thinking."

I hope the distinction is clear. We often think it takes great faith to accomplish great things. But Jesus said: "If ye have faith as a grain of mustard seed, ye shall say unto this mountain, Remove hence to yonder place; and it shall remove; and nothing shall be impossible unto you." (Matt 17:20b) What is Jesus saying? You are not required to have great faith to move mountains only faith as small as the grain of a mustard seed. Not even faith the size of a mustard seed but the "grain" of a mustard seed. That is not much. What is important is in whom you place your faith and hope. Hope in Jesus. Hope in the plan that God has for your life.

Remember the man with the child who had a dumb spirit? (Mark 9:17) "Jesus said unto him, If thou canst believe, all things are possible to him that believeth. And straightway the father of the child cried out, and said with tears, Lord, I believe; HELP THOU MINE UNBELIEF." (Mark 9:23-24) This man did not have great faith. He admitted his lack of faith. He was not thinking positively but he had enough hope to ACT positively and bring his problem to Jesus. (v 17)

There is a story about two condemned prisoners long ago in a dungeon in England. They were scheduled to die the next day. As they hung from their shackles one called to the guard and said. "Go tell the king that if he will grant me two weeks I will teach his horse to talk." Although skeptical the guard agreed to tell the king. The other prisoner said. "What kind of foolishness is this? You can't teach a horse to talk." The prisoner said: "In two weeks I may die. In two weeks the king may die. In two weeks the horse may talk!"

That has been my philosophy. Who knows what God might do if I take a step. Even when I don't think things will work out I still do what has to be done knowing that God may intervene and bring about a positive outcome. The Bible gives many verses about overcoming difficult situations. Here are a few: John 16:33, Rom 12:21, 1 John 5:4-5, and Rev 21:7.

In all these verses God is calling for positive actions. Thinking positively and doing nothing results in failure. I tell young people that if you want to go to Harvard do not think about whether you are likely to achieve that goal. Just go online and get the catalog for Harvard; ask for an application (or now apply online); fill out the application; get the recommendations and submit the application. Just go step by step. Don't look down the road. Don't think about whether you are likely to get in. You are probably not likely to get in. But who knows the horse may talk. If God's plan for your life includes a degree from Harvard you will get a degree from Harvard. God specializes in "doing wonders?" (Ex 15:11)

"Simon Peter, a servant and an apostle of Jesus Christ, to them that have obtained like precious faith with us through the righteousness of God and our Saviour Jesus Christ: Grace and peace be multiplied unto you through the knowledge of God, and of Jesus our Lord, According as his divine power hath given unto us all things that pertain unto life and godliness, through the knowledge of him that hath called us to glory and virtue: Whereby are given unto us exceeding great and precious promises: that by these ye might be partakers of the divine nature, having escaped the corruption that is in the world through lust" (2 Peter 1:1-4).

PRAISE HIM ANYWAY!

"There are two times the devil comes against us; when we do something wrong and when we do something right. So why worry about it either way Jesus is the answer." Joyce Meyer

My wife Rosalynn and I recently returned from a ministerial trip to the Republic of Ireland and Northern Ireland. She was honored to sing and I was honored to preach at the Greater Light International Ministry in Cork City, Ireland. This was our second trip ministering in that country and it was a blessing. However as we boarded the plane to leave for Ireland it did not appear that this was going to be an enjoyable trip. A short time before we were scheduled to leave both my wife and I lost our voices. We had bad colds that resulted in laryngitis. It was terrible. Here we were with all the arrangements made to travel and the hotel reservations made and we were sick. She was scheduled to sing and I was scheduled to preach at the Greater Light International Ministries in Cork City, Ireland and neither of us could even talk. What should we do?

> **"I believed that God would not give me a sermon and not heal me in time to deliver it."**

As the time drew closer the Lord spoke to me in my morning devotion. He told me to write my sermon. I already had a sermon I had planned to preach but God said "write a sermon based on what you are going through." So I started writing but keep in mind that I was writing a sermon at a time when I could not even speak! I did not even know if I would be able to deliver the sermon I was writing. Now I am going to use my two favorite words in the Bible: "BUT GOD" is faithful. That term "But God" is used 44 times in the Bible from Gen 20:3 to 1 Tim 4:8. These are some of the most encouraging verses in the Bible. For example:

"My flesh and my heart faileth: *but God* is the strength of my heart, and my portion forever." (Ps 73:26)

"The righteous man wisely considereth the house of the wicked: *but God* overthroweth the wicked for their wickedness." (Prov. 21:12)

"*But God*, who is rich in mercy, for his great love wherewith he loved us," (Eph 2:4)

"For indeed he was sick nigh unto death: *but God* had mercy on him; and not on him only, but on me also, lest I should have sorrow upon sorrow." (Phil 2:27)

I believed that God would not give me a sermon and not heal me in time to deliver it. The enemy however was saying "Cancel the trip. You know you can't talk. It would be better to cancel the trip now and maybe go later in the summer or next spring." But God continued to speak to me and say "you are going to be blessed and be a blessing on this trip. And this sermon that is born out of your present suffering will bless my people in Cork Ireland who are suffering various attacks and challenges. I am giving you a *rhema* that you can only deliver out of your own pain." God told me there were hurting wounded people in Cork in need of an encouraging word from Him. But they had to know in their souls that I was preaching from the heart and not the mind. They had to feel it so I had to feel it. We all want to be used by God but it is not always a pleasant mountain top experience—at least not at first.

So we boarded the flight to Ireland by faith. I can report that the trip was a blessing above and beyond all we ever imagined. We were received with such love and hospitality that we have no words for it. Every church we visited treated us like special guests. I was blessed to preach and baptize two young people in Cork and lead a young man to the Lord in Belfast. I was honored to briefly speak to the congregation at the great Whitewell Metropolitan Tabernacle a mega church in Belfast. God is always true to His word.

So I completed the sermon and pictured in my mind preaching it to the saints in Cork. The Lord also told me to "praise (Him) and stand on the word of God in the Bible." I shared what I was going through with Evangelist Ratcliff and she told me to "praise God and stand on the word of God in the Bible." That was encouragement and confirmation that all would be well. So my wife and I got on the plane by faith and by Sunday morning I was not 100% but I was able to deliver the sermon that God had given me and the people responded. And Rosalynn was able to sing to the glory of God.

The message I delivered was to praise God in all circumstances. Praise God when you don't feel like praising Him. Make a sacrifice of praise. As it is written: "The voice of joy, and the voice of gladness, the voice of the bridegroom, and the voice of the bride, the voice of them that shall say, *Praise the LORD* of hosts: for the LORD is good; for his mercy endureth for ever: and of them that shall bring the *sacrifice of praise* into the house of the LORD." (Jer. 33:11) "By him therefore, let us offer the *sacrifice of praise* to God continually, that is, the fruit of our lips giving thanks to his name. But to do good and to communicate forget not: for with such sacrifices *God is well pleased*." (Heb 13:15-16)

God inhabits the praises of his people. (Ps 22:3) He expects the praises of those that are experiencing joy and those that are wounded. One circumstance that makes it difficult to praise God is when the wounded person feels that they are to blame for the hurt they are experiencing. I was talking to my doctor about this and she said she thought the opposite was true. She said for example if a person gets lung cancer at least if they knew they were a smoker it would be easier to accept. But I explained that for the Christian it was harder when we believe that our sin brought on our suffering. For those of us that love the Lord it is easier to know we are under attack by the enemy unjustly than to know that we sinned and are suffering the consequences.

And what makes it worse is the devil that tempted us to sin then accuses us of that very sin and tries to convince us that we are unworthy to call on the Lord for help. Satan will tell the suffering person that 'God does not want to hear your praise.' Sometimes the Christian who is suffering feels like Gideon when he said "Oh my Lord, if the LORD be with us, why then is all this befallen us? . . . but now the LORD hath forsaken (me)". (Judg. 6:13)

This is the devil's job as the "accuser of our brethren." He accuses us "before our God day and night." (Rev 12:10) But here is the good news: " . . . our God hath not forsaken us in our bondage, but hath extended mercy unto us." (Ezra 9:9) And we have victory over Satan by "the blood of the Lamb, and by the word of (our) testimony;" (Rev 12:11a) Hurting people need to know: "The LORD is nigh unto them that are of a broken heart; and saveth such as be of a contrite spirit. Many are the afflictions of the righteous: but the LORD delivereth him out of them all." (Ps 34:18-19) Is that not good news?

In addition to fear and guilt there is often in the wounded a feeling of despair; the feeling that my situation is not going to improve and indeed is getting worse. But David said: "He brought me up also out of an *horrible pit*, out of the miry clay, and set my feet upon a rock, and established my goings. And he hath put a new song in my mouth, even praise unto our God: many shall see it, and fear, and shall trust in the LORD." (Ps 40:2-3) Notice that David mentions "praise unto our God." Praise God anyway. Just do it. It works!

Most Christians believe that God loves us but we do not believe that He likes us very much. We tend to think God is angry and disappointed with us most of the time. This is particularly true if we were raised in a strict legalistic church environment—as I was in the Church of Christ. But as the preachers say: "I stopped by to tell you—God not only loves you He LIKES YOU! As David said "(God) *liked me* to make me king over all Israel:" (1 Chron 28:4b) Sure God is sometimes disappointed in us but His love and affection toward His children predominates. So let every Christian praise God. "Let every thing that hath breath praise the LORD. Praise ye the LORD." (Ps 150:6) And wonderful manifestations of His love will follow. As the wounded praise God and experience His love and peace the burden becomes lighter and they know that there is indeed a balm in Gilead. (Jer. 8:22)

LOVE—AS HE IS

Raising children is a complicated and intense experience under normal circumstances. But that experience is relatively simple compared to that of having a child with a disability such as Autism. It involves a love relationship of a most intense nature. The love a parent feels for their child is there before you ever get to "know" the child as a person. Unlike romantic love it is not governed by the behavior of the child or how the child 'treats' the parent. Generally infants are the most demanding of people and do not 'treat' their parents well in the sense that word is often used, but they do have much to teach us as parents. Children whether normal or disabled teach their parents about love.

> *"I am so proud of him when he makes another small step forward in his development."*

Before I became a father I thought I understood the idea of love, but my son brings new dimensions to my understanding of love. Before a person has a child the experience of love is often affected by the behavior of the object of ones love. In romantic love the object of the love can strain or even destroy the emotion by behaving badly. Having a child, particularly a child with a disability redefines all your previous thinking and experience of love. My son Walter has done this for me. Walter is six years old and Autistic. He is also developmentally disabled. With this combination Walter has both the unusual behavior patterns of the Autistic child and he does not speak.

My discussion here will concern my feelings. Not the struggles Rosalynn (my wife) and I have had with the medical and educational systems in our attempts to obtain every possible opportunity and service for Walter. I will say now that it is almost overwhelming that as soon as you learn that your child has a disability you must immediately prepare to fight some of the most frustrating and important battles of your life with the 'system' in order to protect the few rights and obtain the few services available to special children.

It was January 16, 1987 when we learned that Walter's lack of speech is attributable to Autism and Developmental Delay. As with many parents a component of my love for Walter when he was born was my pride. He is so handsome and has few physical signs of his disability. I have hundreds of photos of him which I will show anyone who expresses the slightest interest. Now two years after first learning what the problem is the pride I feel now is so much deeper. I am so proud of him when he makes another small step forward in his development. It is most moving and surprising when he develops a skill, ability or awareness which we have not been attempting to teach or develop. He is full of these surprises. For example he now likes his privacy when he uses the bathroom and he will show this by closing the door. We had not been working on that; how can you. Anyway, that was one of those moments when we can see him progress and the love and pride are felt strongly.

The deeper emotions however are not related to any particular behavior. Indeed sometimes the love is felt despite many of his unusual behavior patterns. I do not love Walter because he can or cannot do any particular thing. I just love Walter. His condition deepens my feelings. It keeps the love closer to the surface and makes it palpable. In the novel "*The World According to Garp*" the main character enjoyed spending entire evenings "watching the kids." I was not a parent when I read that book so I thought that was merely a sweet plot device. I didn't think parents actually did that. I now understand. What is more wonderful than watching your child sleep. Just standing in the door and watching him can bring a lump to my throat. I remember one night he had wet the bed and I had to change the sheets and give him dry clothes. After tucking him in and giving him his pencil (at that time he was fixating on pencils) I just sat by the bed for about half and hour looking at his face. As I watched him fall asleep he was smiling and making the funniest faces. It was a joy.

When I put Walter to bed I like to tell him I love him and that I am so proud of him. He knows the "I love you" part. I do not know if he understands the "I am so proud of you" part but he will smile and touch my lips with the back of his hand when I am talking. He seems to be listening with his hand.

I have thought about how Walter's Autism affects my love for him; I mean, would I feel differently if he were 'normal'. I do not know a Walter who is 'normal'. That would be a different person. I know and love the

Walter who is Autisitc. Shortly after Walter's disability was diagnosed I sometimes wondered why I did not feel a sense of regret at his condition. Of course I wish he did not have disabilities and I want him to develop to his maximum potential; but I do not wish he were different. At first I thought I must be in shock. The 'normal' emotion, I thought' would be to wish Walter were normal. Well intellectually I do; but emotionally I do not know a child named Walter who can talk and attends regular school. I know and love Walter that is my Son and exists as he is. I cannot imagine a child who's development I would take for granted. I know this child who finds ingenious ways to communicate even complex ideas and wishes without speech. I celebrate his abilities rather than regret his disabilities. I love this Walter.

I do not think this is just some sentimental rationalization. When I try to visualize Walter as a 'normal' child I do not see the child I know and love so deeply. His disabilities are part of the person I love. I do not love his Autism but I love him and he has Autism. If he were suddenly not Autistic I would be filled with joy but I would have to get to know this new person.

My point is that being a parent involves loving your child as he or she is. The behavior or personality of the child does not control the love. Nor is it based on his ability to meet societies, friends or families expectations. When your child has a disability I think the love is even less dependant on external factors. It is deep, personal and almost private. You know that society does not understand or experience their love for their children in the same way you do. Your love both is subtle and all consuming. You watch for and rejoice in small accomplishments. You do not take the future for granted.

I do not mean to imply that parents with children with disabilities love their children more than other parents. I do not know. I have one child, Walter and I love him; as he is.

TIMING IS EVERYTHING— HURRY UP AND WAIT!

Here are some thoughts on how God's timing differs from and affects us His children.

DON'T JUMP THE GUN: "*And Moses was learned in all the wisdom of the Egyptians, and was mighty in words and in deeds. And when he was full forty years old, it came into his heart to visit his brethren the children of Israel. And seeing one of them suffer wrong, he defended him, and avenged him that was oppressed, and smote the Egyptian: For he supposed his brethren would have understood how that God by his hand would deliver them: but they understood not. And the next day he showed himself unto them as they strove, and would have set them at one again, saying, Sirs, ye are brethren; why do ye wrong one to another? But he that did his neighbour wrong thrust him away, saying, Who made thee a ruler and a judge over us? Wilt thou kill me, as thou diddest the Egyptian yesterday? Then fled Moses at this saying, and was a stranger in the land of Madian, where he begat two sons.*" (Acts 7:22-28)

We all know this Old Testament story of how Moses killed the Egyptian who was oppressing his Hebrew brother. But it is here in the New Testament we see something interesting in verse 25: "*For he supposed his brethren would have understood how that God by his hand would deliver them: but they understood not.*" Forty years before the burning bush Moses had a revelation that God would use him to deliver Israel and he acted on that belief killing the Egyptian believing the Hebrews would rise up and follow him to freedom. The idea was right but the timing was wrong. Moses was forty years ahead of schedule.

An often-repeated motif in scripture is "wait on the Lord." (Psa. 27:14; 37:34) Indeed Proverbs 20:22 says: "*Say not thou, I will recompense evil; but wait on the LORD, and he shall save thee.*" The time between the call of God to service and the time the service is to begin may be close together or far apart. There may be a season of preparation before the call or an extended time on the backside of the desert after the call. (Gen 2:22; 3:1) There were probably 100 years between God's commission to Noah to build the ark and the flood (Compare Gen 5:32 and 7:6). David was anointed king of Israel many years before he sat on the throne. We do not always know what God is doing or understand His ways or His timing. For God even characterize His actions as strange: "*that he may do his work, his strange work; and bring to pass his act, his strange act.*" (Isaiah 28:21b) Sometimes His strange works take longer than we would prefer. Wait!

> "An often-repeated motif in scripture is "wait on the Lord.""

RECOGNIZE OPPORTUNITIES: So sometimes we are to wait. But sometimes we are to act now. If God has placed you in a position to make a difference now—then act now. Consider Esther whom God placed in the court of King Ahasuerus *"for such a time as this"* to save her people. (Esther 4:14) As the Roman poet Horace said, "*Dump loquimur fugerit invida aetas. Carpe diem quam minimum credula postero.*" Translated: "As we speak jealous time flees. *Seize the day* believing as little as possible in the next." (*Odes* I, 11.8-9)

LISTEN TO THE VOICE OF GOD—NOW: How are we to know when to act or when to wait? God will tell us what to do and when to do it. But we must hear the voice of God accurately and obey specifically. But how do we know for sure we are hearing the voice of God when we are called to a particular service? The same way we know the voice of our earthly fathers, friends and loved ones by spending time talking to and listening to them. We know the voice of God because we talk with Him every day in prayer. We have extended conversations with Him and we have learned that what He says to us proves to be true. Jesus said: "*My sheep hear my voice, and I know them, and they follow me:*" (John 10:27) There should be some time during our devotion when we say "Lord do you have a word for me today?" Then listen.

For me the best time to gather the manna is early in the morning. But there is no wrong time to meet with the Savior. He is always available. He is waiting even right now as I write and later as you read this article. God is waiting right now to talk to us. In fact why not take a few minutes now to ask the Lord if He has a word for you—right now. He has a word we need to get through the next hour or day. Or he has something that we are to give to someone else to help them face a coming time of trial. God truly has an open door policy.

This is critical to ministers because we are not only called to hear God for ourselves but to communicate to His people. We have the awesome responsibility of telling God's people that we have a word from God for them. God takes our role in communicating to His people very seriously. The bible says: *"Dear brothers and sisters, not many of you should become teachers in the church, for we who teach will be judged by God with greater strictness."* (James 3:1 NLT) So our ears must be especially open to hear God distinctly. *"So they read in the book in the law of God distinctly, and gave the sense, and caused them* (the people) *to understand the reading."* (Nehemiah 8:8)

THE END OF TIME: Then there is God's ultimate time. I have tried to think about time from God's point of view. I think everything is present for God. Everything is NOW. Yesterday for us is the present for God. Tomorrow and a thousand tomorrows is still the present for God. As Jesus said: "Before Abraham was, I am." (John 8:58) Not 'I was'; but "I am". Indeed God's very self-designation is "I AM THAT I AM" (Exodus 3:14) the self-existent one. As the writer of Hebrews summed it up: *"Jesus Christ the same yesterday, and to day, and for ever."* (Hebrews 13:8)

No one knows the day or the hour of His return but after Christ reigns for 1000 years on the earth time as we know it will change or cease. In the eternal state I believe we will experience time as God does. Time will be irrelevant. Our memories will not fade over millions of years so all time will be present. As the song says: "When we've been here ten thousand years . . . bright shining as the sun. We've no less days to sing God's praise . . . than when we've first begun." Now that's worth waiting for.

THE MAN ON THE PORCH

In 1969 after returning home from Vietnam I got a job loading and unloading trucks for the Dresher Mfg. Co. at 13th and Kostner on the west side of Chicago. It was a hard job and I worked factory hours starting at 7am. During this time I bought a life insurance policy from the Prudential Ins. Co. The agent, who sold me the policy Mr. Green, believed I had potential as an insurance agent (salesman). It sounded good to me—anything that would get me out of that factory sounded good to me. So I completed the application and Mr. Green and the other agents were very enthusiastic about my prospects.

After being accepted into the training program the first thing I had to do was make a list of my friends whom I would contact under their supervision and attempt to sell them life insurance. My list had about three or four names on it. And I was not excited about bothering them about life insurance. Mr. Green was very disappointed. He could not believe I had so few friends. I did not become an insurance agent I continued to unload trucks at Dresher. The problem was that I have been a loner all my life. I have never had many friends and I am not a joiner of clubs or associations. So I was not salesman material.

Recently I watched a movie called *The Big Kahuna* staring Kevin Spacey, Danny DeVito and Peter Facinelli. These characters were salesmen who were trying to sell industrial lubricants to a big potential client they called the Big Kahuna. The Facinelli character, a Christian, managed to meet and have several extended conversations with the Big Kahuna but rather than try to sell him industrial lubricants he talked to the man about Jesus. This really irritated Spacey and DeVito. They needed to make the sale to the Big Kahuna or face the loss of their jobs. But Facinelli did not feel it was right to mix selling with witnessing. Near the end of the movie DeVito tells Facinelli that his talking to the Kahuna about Jesus with the intent to convert him or save him was in fact selling. He said Facinelli was selling Jesus just like Spacey was selling industrial lubricants. DeVito's point was that as soon as the conversation turned from just talk to a conscious effort to point the other person to Christ that was selling not talking.

I sometimes watch a program on CNBC called *High Net Worth*. The last time I watched it the host Tyler Mathisen interviewed John Paul Dejoria the cofounder of the Paul Mitchell hair care products company. Mathisen ask him what is the basis of your success. Mr. Dejoria said you have to love your product. You have to believe you are selling something that will enhance people's lives. I have heard this idea before and I agree with it. In fact most great business men or women or athletes or entertainers excelled because they were doing something they loved. I have heard that Michael Jordan had a "love-of-the-game" clause in his contract with the Bulls that allowed him to play basketball in the off-season. Michael did not love basketball because he was good at it—he was good at it because he loved it.

A few days ago a contractor came to my home to give me an estimate on some roofing work. After looking at the roof we talked on the front porch and the conversation stretched to about two hours. And as is usually the case in any conversation of any length I began talking about Jesus. And at one point this man asks me "what does it mean to be saved?" Later he said "isn't Christianity a crutch?" I said yes it is a wonderful crutch. When your leg is broken you need a crutch. Jesus is a great crutch for the heartsick soul. And so the conversation went. As I talked I was praying for wisdom to present Christ in the most effective way.

I often have conversations like that. In my professional work I sometimes serve with other lawyers on panels hearing personal injury liability cases. There is a lot of time to talk and when I mention that I am a minister that usually leads to a conversation about religion and Jesus. My ears are always tuned to hear any sign that the other person may be interested in hearing the Gospel.

So what is the common thread that runs through these varied situations I have described? Personal evangelism is selling. And like any successful selling you must love your 'product.' You must believe your 'product' Jesus adds value to peoples' lives. There are courses and web cites devoted to teaching Christians how to evangelize. I am looking at one (*www.netbiblestudy.net/evangelism/*) as I write that covers such topics as: "Sources of Prospects", "What To Say", "Persuasion", "Closing", "Handling Objections" etc. That sure sounds like selling to me.

In my own life I have never found any thing, idea or experience that has taken me out of my self absorption until Jesus came into my life. Whereas before I avoided social contact with people I now seek them out in order to present Christ. I have 'led' several of my friends to Christ. Jesus transforms every life in unique ways and this is one way He has affected mine. So I guess I have come full circle because whereas I did not want to "bother" my friends about Prudential life insurance I love selling the only real eternal life insurance on the market. Jesus the Christ.

CHANGE MAY TAKE TIME

An old hymn says: "What a wonderful change in my life has been wrought Since Jesus came into my heart! I have ceased from my wondering and going astray, Since Jesus came into my heart!"

Indeed there are wonderful changes when Jesus comes into our lives. But have you ever "led" someone to Christ and then felt frustration when you did not see much real change in his or her life. I have! You witnessed to your friend, relative, acquaintance or coworker etc. The person expresses remorse about their sinful life and prays the 'sinner's prayer' asking Jesus to come in and be Lord of their life. But then nothing. Either they will not attend church regularly. Or perhaps they did get baptized and filled with the Holy Spirit but you still see no appreciable change in their lifestyle.

I have been blessed to witness to and lead several of my friends to the Lord. All of them were moved to respond to my witness because they saw the changes God made in my life. These are people who "knew me when." So when they saw that I changed dramatically and that I was happy in my new life they were moved to listen to my testimony. But some have manifested very little change that I can see in their lives.

Recently I read an article in Christianity Today magazine titled Am*azing Sin, How Deep We're Bound*. In this article the author Mark R. McMinn describes the conversion of John Newton the author of the great hymn *Amazing Grace*. We have all heard the story of how Newton was converted in the midst of a raging storm at sea while transporting slaves. It is a great story. What is less well known is that though his conversion was immediate his behavior changed very little for years. Right after his conversion he signed on to another slave ship and went to Africa traveling from village to village buying more salves. He then sailed across the Atlantic, studying a Latin Bible in his quarters as 200 slaves lay shackled in the hull of the ship.

Upon arriving in Charleston, SC Newton delivered these men, women and children into a life of slavery and then attended church.

Even though Newton began writing letters and journal entries that showed pity for his human cargo he did not change his profession or behavior. He even became captain of his own slave ships and he continued to steal and sell human lives for several more years. Newton's slave trading might have continued for many more years except for a seizure that made a career change medically necessary. In all, Newton spent 10 years trading slaves, most of them *after* his conversion to Christianity.

Yet at the end of his life Newton's epitaph on his gravestone reads: "John Newton, clerk, once an infidel and libertine, a servant of slaves in Africa, was, by the rich mercy of our Lord and Saviour Jesus Christ, preserved, restored, pardoned, and appointed to preach the faith he had long laboured to destroy."

Salvation is instantaneous. Regeneration, redemption, justification, propitiation all happen in an instant if indeed these spiritual acts can be quantified by time. These are instantaneous sovereign works of God. But Sanctification, which is becoming Christ like in behavior, happens over time and continues throughout the Christian life. As ministers we preach and teach the Good News but it is the Holy Spirit that quickens (John 6:63; cf 1 Timothy 6:13; Romans 8:11) the sinner and moves him to be more Christ like in his or her life. Strongholds are constantly revealed and overcome by the power of the Holy Spirit in our lives. Every time I think I have a handle on one sin the Holy Spirit sensitizes me to another area that needs attention. Changes come by prayer, experience, bible study and the countless ways God speaks his will into our hearts.

I have to remember that change even after salvation sometimes comes the hard way. Sometimes I have had to experience some divine chastening to really let some vestiges of the world go. Not all changes happen overnight. In fact recently I was reading my journal from the time I came to the Lord. And I can see that not all the changes in my life were as fast as I remember. I was still cursing months after being filled with the Holy Spirit. Other habits took a long time to wane. But memory truncates these changes to make them appear to have happened in a shorter period than they actually happened. I just have to thank God for his new mercies every day. For *"This I recall to my mind, therefore have I hope. It is of the LORD's mercies that we are not consumed, because his compassions fail not. They are new every morning: great is thy faithfulness."* (Lam 3:21-23) So I will pray for my newly converted friends and be as patient with them as God is with me.

www.ingramcontent.com/pod-product-compliance
Lightning Source LLC
Chambersburg PA
CBHW031254280526
45784CB00004B/1852